JAMES'S *THE TURN OF THE SCREW*

Continuum *Reader's Guides*

Continuum *Reader's Guides* are clear, concise and accessible introductions to classic literary texts. Each book explores the themes, context, criticism and influence of key works, providing a practical introduction to close reading and guiding the reader towards a thorough understanding of the text. Ideal for undergraduate students, the guides provide an essential resource for anyone who needs to get to grips with a literary text.

JAMES'S *THE TURN OF THE SCREW*

A READER'S GUIDE

LEONARD ORR

continuum

Continuum International Publishing Group

Continuum London	Continuum New York
The Tower Building	80 Maiden Lane, Suite 704
11 York Road	New York
London SE1 7NX	NY 10038

www.continuumbooks.com

British Library Cataloguing-in-Publication Data
A catalogue record for this book is available from the British Library.

ISBN: 978-0-8264-3019-9 (hardback)
       978-0-8264-2432-7 (paperback)

Library of Congress Cataloging-in-Publication Data
A catalog record for this book is available from the Library of Congress.

Typeset by Newgen Imaging Systems Pvt. Ltd, Chennai, India
Printed and bound in Great Britain by MPG Books Ltd,
Bodmin, Cornwall

CONTENTS

QUOTATIONS AND ABBREVIATIONS

All references to *The Turn of the Screw* are to the 2004 Bedford/ St. Martin's edition in the Case Studies series (indicated by the abbreviation of *TotS*). All of the scholarly texts below, the most commonly used editions, are based on the same copy text, James's New York Edition volume 12, published in 1908. While many scholarly works use the page references to the 1908 work, I am following this practice (which is also common in many recent books and articles including the 2005 MLA guide for instructors teaching the work) because it is unlikely the audience for this work will be using that earlier edition, now a century old. The paperback editions go in and out of print and the page numbers change from one edition to the next. I have tried to prepare for this by having all quotations from the text first appear with a chapter number (which is the same in all editions, followed by the page number). A quotation or reference to page 53 of the Bedford/St. Martin's edition would be written in the parenthetical in-text reference as (*TotS* 6: 53). In any other edition, it is in chapter 6. Sometimes I use one or the other major texts, the Norton Critical Edition or the Oxford World Classic edition are indicated by abbreviations.

TotS   Henry James, *The Turn of the Screw.* Case Studies in Contemporary Criticism, second edition. Peter G. Beidler, ed. Boston and New York: Bedford/St. Martin's, 2004.

NCE   Henry James, *The Turn of the Screw.* A Norton Critical Edition, second edition. Deborah Esch and Jonathan Warren, eds. New York: W. W. Norton, 1999.

OWC   Henry James, *The Turn of the Screw and Other Stories.* T. J. Lustig, ed. Oxford World Classics. Oxford and New York: Oxford University Press 1992, reissued, 2008.

CHAPTER 1

CONTEXTS

BIOGRAPHY

The James Family

Henry James was born on April 15, 1843, in New York City into a highly eccentric family, one that was immediately crossing boundaries and borders and was outside of the mainstream of settled life and expectations, transatlantic and yet deeply rooted in American culture and issues. The family included four authors and they have been analyzed intensively both as individuals and in their interrelations. Through the nineteenth century the family fortune diminished, as in a Victorian novel, with an encumbered will, lawsuits to break the will, and the attempt by the founder of the family, a real estate developer, to reach beyond the grave to force his seemingly wastrel children (thirteen from three marriages) to take up professions and appropriate work. William James, Henry's grandfather, left $3,000,000 when he died in 1832. Henry's father is also named Henry and referred to hereafter as Henry Sr.; Henry kept the "Jr." until his father's death in 1882. After his lawsuit, Henry Sr. received an annual payment of $10,000 a year. This was a large amount in the 1840s, placing the family socially among the wealthy, and allowing for the travel and odd schooling, as well as for the freedom to do as they wished. By the time he died, there was little left of the fortune.

Henry Sr. married Mary Robertson Walsh and had five children. Henry's closest sibling was William (1842–1910); his younger siblings were Garth Wilkinson (1845–1883), Robertson (1846–1910), and Alice (1848–1892). When Henry was still an infant, the family moved to England for a year. This first European journey was cut short by Henry Sr.'s nervous breakdown following a frightening vision he described as a "vastation," and the family rushed back to Albany and eventually New York City again. The family history is marked by such breakdowns, reports of mysterious and perhaps psychosomatic or hypochondriac illnesses, strange injuries and "obscure hurts," suicidal depression, financial problems and failed business schemes, and, in the case of Robertson, alcoholism. Alice remained unmarried and a chronic invalid but shown by her letters and remarkable diary to be deeply perspicacious and observant.

While Mary is described as attentive and involved with all of the members of the family and especially a support to her husband through all of his changes, family moves, and intellectual projects, Henry Sr. was a force of nature. His battles with his father perhaps made him decisive and aggressive but not in the realm of business. Despite a stutter (and having a leg amputated at the age of 13 when he was accidentally set on fire during a hot-air balloon experiment), he argued and lectured loudly and enthusiastically. He was deeply interested in theology although brought up as a Presbyterian, he studied Unitarianism and thought of becoming a minister; he hosted the Transcendentalists Ralph Waldo Emerson, Henry David Thoreau, and others during their New York visits. He was drawn to Christian Primitivism and rejected the mainstream churches. After the mystical experience of his "vastation," he became a dedicated Swedenborgian and wrote a number of books and lectured widely on the topic. But he also rejected the organized Swedenborgian congregations, developing his own Christian Socialism. He was an active abolitionist before the Civil War and had strong views on topics ranging from property to education, from social justice to hidden symbols behind the words of scriptures.

William was seen by Henry and others as the most impressive and successful of the James family. Throughout their lives, William and Henry watched and criticized each other's work, and studied each other's many publications to find both influences and common ground. They shared the consequence of the constant moves both within New York and in Europe (including one three-year stay when Henry was 15). They went to at least ten schools and many tutors; they went to art galleries and museums and became fluent in Italian, French, and German. They had extended stays in England, France, Venice, Rome, and Switzerland. William first intended to become an artist but switched to the sciences. He studied medicine at Harvard University (receiving the M.D. in 1869), became a professor of Physiology and Philosophy and was one of the creators of the academic discipline of Psychology, writing the major textbook in the field, the two-volume *The Principles of Psychology* (1890). In philosophy, he was identified with pragmatism along with thinkers such as Charles Peirce and John Dewey. His other major works include *The Will to Believe* (1897), *Pragmatism* (1907), *The Varieties of Religious Experience* (1907), *A Pluralistic Universe* (1909).

By contrast with the activist and argumentative Henry Sr. and the Harvard-credentialed professor with an international influence, his brother William, Henry did not receive any degrees, did not attend college except for a very brief experiment in Harvard Law School, but launched himself into the risky life of a freelance writer of fiction and literary essays. For several years, coinciding with the Civil War (which he was able to avoid through a back injury; the two younger brothers served in two black Massachusetts regiments and Wilkerson was seriously wounded in battle), he had been in secret preparation, practicing writing and studying literature from several nations and languages, for what he saw as his natural career. His first book reviews and short stories began to appear in journals when he was in his early twenties.

Henry James claimed that his earliest memory was as an infant during a visit to Paris and seeing the column in the Place Vendôme in honor of Napoleon; the constant shifts of residence around Europe, from New York to London or Paris or Geneva, within the different cities, became a permanent feature for Henry in a way they did not for the other Jameses. They settled somewhere and bought properties (William even had a summer property of 25 acres with 2 houses and a barn on Chocorua Lake in New Hampshire). Until he was almost 55 years old, Henry lived in hotels, rooms at elegant clubs, in the guest rooms of his friends' properties, or visiting the homes of his extended family. He made the great leap of buying Lamb House in Rye, Sussex in 1897. From the end of the 1860s, James was primarily an expatriate, returning only occasionally and for family reasons; in the last 50 years of his life, he was always conscious of his estrangement from America (described especially in *The American Scene* [1907]), written after a 25-year absence from his home country. In Europe, though he was multilingual and widely read, he was aware of being an American among Europeans, the subject of the so-called international theme mentioned often in connection with his work.

James's life was both constantly social and intensely private. In his family circle he had become acquainted with many American intellectual luminaries (in addition of Emerson and Thoreau, William Cullen Bryant, Bronson Alcott, Washington Irving, and Oliver Wendell Holmes), prominent artists such as William Morris Hunt, and of course anyone drawn into the house for argument with Henry Sr. over socialism or religion. When he was resident in Europe, he guided the visiting Americans through museums or tourist sites. He came to know Charles Darwin, William Morris, Leslie Stephen (editor of the *Dictionary of National Biography* and father of Virginia Woolf), Gustave Flaubert, Ivan Turgenev, Émile Zola, Alphonse Daudet, Robert Louis Stevenson, Edmund Gosse, John Singer Sargent, Theodore Roosevelt, W. E. Gladstone, James McNeill Whistler, and on and on. He knew people whose world was in politics, in theater, and in medicine. He kept up with the innumerable second and third cousins and their children. He attended the theater and opera and art exhibitions. More than 10,000 letters of his survive despite his requests to his correspondents that they destroy any of his letters in their possession. A wholly new edition of his complete letters is now being published for the first time; the first two volumes appeared in 2006 of what is projected to fill 140 volumes (see Walker 2000; Walker and Zacharias 2006, 2007).

The recent unveiling of these thousands of letters, coinciding with the development of gender studies, gay studies, and, more recently, queer studies, has made the question of James's sexuality one of the most active areas of critical and biographical work on James. He never married and there still are no direct statements establishing that he had sexual relations with anyone, man or woman. Recently there have been collections published of passionately phrased letters to younger men and certainly he had friendships with prominent homosexuals in England (see Gunter and Jobe 2001). But the issue is complicated by his similarly phrased letters to a number of women. Recent biographers are quick to see homosexual liaisons or at least "falling in love" with men throughout James's life in the same way earlier biographers speculated about heterosexual love stories; the lack of direct statement by James is taken to be proof of his self-repression. This will be taken up in Chapters 3 and 4.

Beginning in 1897, coinciding with his failed attempt at playwriting and about the time he started *The Turn of the Screw*, James suffered what would now be called carpal tunnel syndrome from all those hours and decades spent in writing in longhand all of those manuscripts and letters as well as his notebooks. He changed his working methods, purchased a typewriter, and hired an ex-army stenographer and typist to operate this cutting-edge technology. It required him to work in the presence of this other person instead of in solitude, to be composing during set hours and in a fixed place, and to dictate his words (despite his stutter). This great change in his working habits proved surprisingly conducive to James; he enjoyed hours of dictation typed up almost immediately for him to revise and then have the revisions retyped. He was able to stride instead of sit and hear, as if from a stage, his words said slowly; he could revise as he spoke, but because he pronounced every punctuation mark, this led to dispensing with superfluous punctuation (one of the major changes he made to earlier texts when he revised them for the New York Edition of his collected works).

James's health began to deteriorate after 1909 with gout and then a nervous breakdown in 1910 (followed that year by the deaths of both his younger brother Robertson and his older brother William), and shingles in 1912. Despite illness, he was publicly active and honored. He received honorary degrees from Harvard and Oxford Universities and, at the start of World War I in 1914, chaired the American Volunteer Motor Ambulance Corps in France, raised money for war relief, and did volunteer work for the wounded. He learned, in 1915, that as a citizen of still-neutral America, he was an alien. He could not go to his home in coastal Rye without registering with the police. He applied for British citizenship and received it at once (Lord Asquith is one of his sponsors). In December he suffered two strokes just before he was awarded the Order of Merit by King George V. He died on February 28, 1916, and his ashes were buried in the James family plot in Cambridge, Massachusetts.

The Writing Life

In his 50-year span of professional writing, James published 22 novels (the last 2 incomplete at the time of his death), 112 stories, many of novella length), many volumes of biography and autobiography, books of travel, a steady stream of essays and book reviews. It is conventional in James criticism to divide this prolific career into periods: the Early (1864–1880), the Middle (1881–1890), the Experimental (1891–1900), and the Late (1901–1904, the date of the last completed novel, *The Golden Bowl*). Any periodization is problematic, whether for literary histories or for nations. It can be misleading in seeming to be with clearly fixed boundaries and firm breaks and not illustrating the numerous continuities that unifies the entire *oeuvre* of any one author. However, just as the student of geology will just have to understand and accept the uses of the terms Triassic, Holocene, and Cretaceous, this is not the place to present arguments about the way James criticism has sorted out his work.

Throughout his career, James was simultaneously writing fiction, essays on other writers, and travel journalism. The nonfiction informs the fiction, entering into the settings, sometimes displaying the influences of other more established or foreign authors he was reading, or showing his developing ideas about fiction, especially the novel (soon reprinted in collections such as *Transatlantic Sketches* [1875] or *French Poets and Novelists* [1878]). In the early work, he published more than thirty stories in the leading British and American journals, as well as seven novels. He was trying out all of the popular forms and sometimes writing in direct response to another author's poorly achieved story. He sometimes wrote stories that were variations of the same plot and he recorded in his notebooks ideas or originating anecdotes. Not surprisingly, this resulted in some novels and stories he did not want to keep among his works (such as his first novel, *Watch and Ward* [1871]). But he also published such enduringly popular novels as *Daisy Miller* (1878) and *Washington Square* (1880). In his work of the 1870s, through such stories as "A Passionate Pilgrim," "Madame de Mauves," and "The Last of the Valerii" and in the novels *Roderick Hudson, The American,* and *The Europeans,* James consistently returned to what is often called the "international theme." Here we can see consistency with his life and nonfiction: he was a nexus of cultural conflicts, of Old European aristocracy, wealthy Americans, and tourists or expatriates scattered through Europe. His essays presented European and American literature to the British, British authors and Old World culture to Americans, and chronicled the clashes and confusions, stereotypes and thwarted relationships, that occurred with the new money, new mobility, and class-climbing. In a letter to English writer Edmund Gosse, James noted that "Nothing at this hour would give me more pleasure than if an intelligent stranger, deigning to cast a glance on my productions, should say that he was mystified—couldn't tell whether they are the work of an American writing about England or of an Englishman writing about America" (Moore 1988: 59).

During the 1880s, the middle period, James produced his first great popular and critical success (*The Portrait of a Lady* [1881]) and some of his most enduring stories (notably "The Aspern Papers," "The Author of Beltraffio"). These works indicate James's interest in moving beyond conventions of Victorian fiction toward the Realism and Naturalism he admired in French authors (especially Émile Zola, Honoré de Balzac, and Alphonse Daudet). At the same time, he was repelled by the new realists representation of sex and violence, didacticism, and by their blunter and sometimes tedious style, filled with facts and displays of research but not sufficiently artful. *The Portrait of a Lady* has attracted readers and critics because of the complexity of the main character, Isabel Archer, the fullness of her thinking, the elegance of the style, and because of the formal elements that incorporate symmetry and elaborate structural parallels that would have particular appeal to James's modernist readers. The series of novels later in the decade (*The Princess Casamassima* and *The Bostonians* [both 1886] and *The Tragic Muse* [1890]) are much more problematic; they were poorly received and the sales were so discouraging James thought he was finished with fiction and, for a time, turned to trying to make a career in the theater. These novels strike many readers as being less controlled, switching mode from realism to satire, having unmotivated or overly simplistic characters, and by uninformed and unconvincing portrayals of feminism, anarchism, and political terrorism.

For the first five years of the 1890s, James dedicated himself to playwriting and the study of drama (especially the plays of Henrik Ibsen). After being booed by some in the audience at the opening of his play *Guy Domville*, James reassessed his relation to fiction and all that he learned from attempting dramatic construction and dialogue. The work that poured out during the "experimental period" represent a shift to concentrated form following a "scenario" with exposition, rising action, complications, climax, and denouement. It may seem odd to think of this structural plan (that goes back to Aristotle's *Poetics*) as something experimental, but in James's understanding it becomes fluid and organic rather than mechanical. The works develop their own surprises for the author even after the scenario; they grow beyond the expected length, minor characters become the major character, and the narrative focus can be altered. Surprisingly, for someone who was recovering from the shock of critical failures and low sales, James's style becomes marked by indirection, by hesitation, silence, and narrative gaps, and by ambiguities; the works become more challenging to the reader, not less. The works of the experimental period include *The Awkward Age*, *The Spoils of Poynton*, *What Maisie Knew*, *The Sacred Fount*, "The Figure in the Carpet," "In the Cage," and, of course, *The Turn of the Screw* (1898). Most of these works are set solely in England and are often focused on women and children in distressed or dysfunctional families, and the decadence of the aristocracy and British society.

James's late phase had a retrospective tinge; he wrote three autobiographical volumes and edited his collected works (another venture that had disappointingly small sales). The New York Edition not only was a matter of selection and compilation but of frequent revision and of composition. He rewrote the works, especially the earlier pieces, into conformity with his later style. He wrote the prefaces to all of the volumes (sometimes meandering and perhaps evasive analysis, sometimes explaining the anecdotes or overheard events that sparked the original story, other times, he considers the techniques or forms he employed). He completed three novels between 1901 and 1904: *The Ambassadors*, *The Wings of the Dove*, and *The Golden Bowl*. These works continue the stylistic trajectory started with the experimental phase; these works are characterized by long, convoluted, complex sentences with appositive phrases and multiple clauses, self-interruption and correction, and ambiguity. The actions in plots are reduced while the consciousness of the characters is highlighted bringing late James closer to the modernist authors than the Victorian or Naturalist models he had followed earlier. Although these late works can at first frustrate and baffle, they are the works that most solidified James's reputation as "The Master."

CONTEXTS

Historical

Considering James's biography and his written works (even his travel writing and autobiographies), it is sometimes difficult to realize what momentous changes were occurring in world politics and power. The United States in 1843, the year of James's birth, was largely agricultural, mainly unsettled, with much of the western part of the country still territories and not states, and the major issue of the time was slavery and the conflicts and compromises that would lead to the

Civil War (1861–1865). His father and the family's large social circle was actively involved in the Abolitionist movement, his two younger brothers, as we noted earlier, served as officers with Union units of black soldiers, and older brother William, finishing his medical studies, volunteered in treating the war wounded. James began writing stories while the war was still raging, but he did not draw upon it for his works of fiction. In the half-century after the Civil War, the United States began its transformation to the world power it would become in the twentieth century. It completed its settlement of the continental 48 states (destroying or displacing the Native Americans), accepted millions of immigrants from Europe fleeing the Irish Potato Famine, the Russian pogroms, the civil wars in Italy, or else those seeking jobs or land. The defeat of Spain in the Spanish-American War of 1898 made the United States a fledgling empire in possession of the Philippines, Puerto Rico, Guam (soon to add Cuba, American Samoa, and the U.S. Virgin Islands). The United States population at the time of his birth was about seventeen million (the Census not counting the nearly four million slaves at the start of the Civil War). By the time of the 1920 Census, three years after James's death, the nation's population was 106 million.

The Europe that became James's home for 50 years was shifting dramatically as well. The "old powers" were in constant contention to maintain or expand their colonial holdings and ward off the young powers (Germany after its unification in 1871 and the post–Civil War United States). When James arrived in mid-century England, the population of London was about three million and it was the center of the largest empire in history. By 1900, the British Empire occupied four million square miles. But this was not an easy position; British forces were at war somewhere in the world every year of Queen Victoria's reign. Queen Victoria's longevity (she lived from 1819–1901 and was crowned in 1837, and Empress of India in 1876) turned into a symbol of the feeble condition of England. She wore mourning for 50 years and removed herself from public life following Prince Albert's death. The debacle of the Second Boer War (1899–1902), the longest, most expensive, and most unpopular Imperial war of the century marks the diminishment of the Empire through the 1950s. It was a punishing guerilla war with a tiny country fighting the largest and technologically advanced army in the world. The death of Queen Victoria in the middle of this war, together with the "fin-de-siècle" consciousness as the century approached its ominous double-zeros, was clearly part of the psychological malaise that effected the British self-confidence. King Edward would have only a seven-year reign and shortly after that, all of the powers were drawn into World War I (1914–1919).

James wrote comparatively little about world events but those essays have been usefully collected by Pierre Walker in *Henry James on Culture* (1999). As London correspondent for the American journal *The Nation*, James contributed articles on the Second Afghan War and about the Zulu defeat of the British at Usandhlwana, Natal, as well as the Russo-Turkish War. At the close of his life, he could not focus on his fiction or literary essays. He wrote six articles, found in Walker's collection, on the start of the World War, the wounded, and the refugees, and spent all his time (in a period of declining health) trying to assist the causes, while the United States was still neutral.

Intellectual

With such a cosmopolitan figure as James, it is hard to capture in a short space what might be considered the "intellectual context." It would vary considerably whether we examine the United States, Europe (broadly to include his various residencies and his reading in several languages), as well as the impact of reading the works of his brother and so introduced to a wide range of current philosophy and the nascent field of psychology. We have noted that he was on the fringes of American intellectual circles since he grew up within Emerson's Transcendentalism mixed with his father's highly individual thinking and mysticism. (For a fine one-volume summary of the Victorian contexts see Philip Davis 2002).

In the first part of the century, geological study of fossils began undercutting what was the biblical account of the origins of humans and the animals, revealing that animals and plants flourished and became extinct, and that there were many layers of changes that represent perhaps millions of years of time and not the 7,000 years that fit the "Mosaic Cosmogony." Charles Lyell's *Principles of Geology* (1830–1833) and other works in this new science prepared a receptive audience for Charles Darwin's *Origin of the Species* (1859). Theologians and evangelical amateur scientists attempted to reconcile the biblical chronology with evolution and the fossil evidence.

There is behind this discourse a desire for spirituality and something supernatural, even where some (such as Matthew Arnold or

Walter Pater) offered intense aesthetic experience, delight in the apprehension of the beautiful or the romantic sublime, instead of the traditional theology. This was developed into a secular ethicism: the important thing was righteous action, conducting oneself in accord with the universal notions of good. This is the sort of argument developed in William James's *Varieties of Spiritual Experience* and *The Will-to-Believe*. His argument is that if our desire to believe in God causes us to conduct our lives well, it does not matter whether God actually exists. Henry James declared himself to be already in accord with his brother's pragmatistic philosophy when he read it (his only essay on the topic was written in response to a journal's request for guest authors to comment on the existence of life after death).

Cultural

Related to this issue of the desire for the spiritual outside of organized religion (and relevant to *The Turn of the Screw*) is the general interest in the second half of the Victorian period in ghosts and the supernatural. Although the traditional churches were losing authority, there was a renewed interest in séances, reports of haunted houses, and spirit guides speaking through mediums who practiced automatic writing while they were in trances. The mysterious Madam Blavatsky founded the Theosophical Society in 1875 to impart the ancient teachings of the yogis and Eastern savants. In 1882, the Society for Psychical Research was founded to investigate and document the many reports of ghost sightings and other supernatural events and visitations. William James was an active member and contributor to this group, sending reports from the American chapter to the London chapter. On one occasion, he had Henry read his report to the Society for Psychical Research (SPR). Peter Beidler, Martha Banta, and T. J. Lustig have documented the way echoes of case histories appearing in the SPR reports and in the popular magazine *Borderland* can be found in *The Turn of the Screw*.

Perhaps the most conflicted, and paradoxically most repressed and argued, context to mention involves gender, sexual practice, and identity, masculinity and femininity. Sexuality and passions were condemned in the Victorian period while, hypocritically, prostitution flourished, women and children were abused, and pornography was collected and sold. In the years immediately before the composition of *The Turn of the Screw*, "the love that dare not speak its name," homosexuality, was brought to loud public attention in the arrest and trial of Oscar Wilde for his liaison with Lord Alfred Douglas.

Literary

Henry James stands on the cusp of Victorian and Modernism, British and American, Continental literatures and work produced in English. He was a working writer who was concerned with the changing markets, the tastes of the audiences (never achieving "best-selling" status); at the same time, he was interested in the theory of fiction generally and the shifting notions of realism and effect. Generalizing very broadly, the Victorian novel emphasized plot and all other elements were to contribute to the success of the plot. The plot was to have exposition, rising action, complications and reversals, a climax, and brief unraveling or denouement. The characters, style, setting, duration, and other elements were all serving the plot. But ever since Daniel Defoe at the beginning of the eighteenth century, the novel was seen as connected to realism: reflecting the lives, relationships, and of the time. What constituted both accurate reflection of society and acceptable representation and candor changed through the decades of the nineteenth century (as it has continued to change to the present, even as the discussion shifted from novels to films or songs or art works). The prevailing belief that art should be higher than life was in conflict with the professed goal of mirroring society. Victorian novels tightly controlled their readers to make certain they followed the complicated stories and reached the correct judgment of the characters and their actions (often with a commenting, omniscient third-person narrator and periodic summaries or reminders when characters reappeared after long absences, a consequence of the practice of serialization). The work often had an epilogue to explain how poetic justice prevailed in the years following the end of the plot with all of the characters (the best example of this sort of epilogue is in George Eliot's *Middlemarch* [1871–1872]).

The novel became the major literary form in the Victorian period with the great increase of the middle class, with the steam-powered presses, linotype machines, and wood-pulp paper making books affordable to the "mass market" for the first time, and with the proliferation of journals that published novels serially prior to book publication. The impact of these on the actual form and content of fiction can be debated, but certainly it created genre expectations, and an idea of the novelist as a craftsman serving the market (as opposed to the Romantic idea of writing out of inspiration). The many changes in James's writing, outlined above, shows his willingness, on the one hand, to fit in with the changing interests of audiences and editors through time, and, on the other hand, to deviate from this, to experiment, and rebel from what he saw us not only increasingly unrealistic but inartistic. The Victorian novel was a capacious field (add to this James's multilingual American and Continental reading). He studied the novels of aristocratic society, the sensation fiction, ghost stories, social change novels, works of naturalism (realism and determinism). In his 1908 preface to *The Tragic Muse* (1889) we see the shift. Twentieth-century James sees the work of Victorian James and classes it along with novels by William Makepeace Thackeray, Alexandre Dumas, and Leo Tolstoy, asking "but what do such large loose baggy monsters, with their queer elements of the accidental and the arbitrary, artistically *mean*?" James admits instead his "delight in a deep-breathing economy and an organic form. . . . I urge myself to the candid confession that in very few of my productions, to my eye, *has* the organic centre succeeded in getting into proper position" (James, *French Writers* 1984: 1107, 1108). What James found instead of end-directed focus on plot and predictable form was concentration on characters' perceptions, shifting "centers of consciousness," and following the flow of thoughts named first by William James as "rivers of consciousness" in his textbook on psychology, transformed by Henri Bergson into *élan vital*, returning to English as stream-of-consciousness and durational flux. James's later fiction is credited by most historians of the subject as one of the foundations of modernist aesthetics, noting James's influence on James Joyce, Virginia Woolf, Dorothy Richardson, T. S. Eliot, and others (see Childs 2000: 74–85; Stevenson 1992: 18–21; Trotter 1999: chapter 3).

QUESTIONS

1. Read at least two of the short works James published around the same time as *The Turn of the Screw* (such as *What Maisie Knew*, "The Figure in the Carpet," or "In the Cage"). None of these are ghost stories but they have common elements. What are these and how does knowing these other works alter or strengthen your reading of *The Turn of the Screw*?

2. How are changes in literary and artistic movements in Britain from 1880–1920 effected by (or are responses to) outside events such as war, new technologies, class conflicts, or gender roles?
3. What were the popular and medical understandings of madness and hysteria during the late Victorian period? How were the insane or depressed treated by physicians?

CHAPTER 2

LANGUAGE, STYLE, AND FORM

LANGUAGE

No other author can be mistaken for Henry James during his experimental or late phase; his sentences and patterns are uniquely in his voice. James stands as a transitional writer at the end of the Victorian period and the cusp of modernism and his work had a deep influence on the British and American avant-garde in the first quarter of the twentieth century. Along with such modernists as James Joyce, Joseph Conrad, or Virginia Woolf, James's increasing push into nonnormative prose and other techniques ran counter to his often-repeated search for popular success. With any such authors, grouped under the inadequate term "experimental," it is worthwhile considering why authors who were capable of writing plainly would develop styles that would cause resistance in readers, that would violate the normal expectations of easy consumption and comprehension, and in some ways force readers to be challenged by their texts.

Although the first response of readers of James's later work, even a century later, may be bafflement or exasperation, it is best to stay with it and keep going. *The Turn of the Screw* was not published for an audience of trained, twenty-first-century literary critics who had many different critical approaches ready to deploy, who were well-versed in deconstruction, postcolonialism, and psychoanalytic methods. It was published in a general magazine as an entertainment, a ghost story, and was James's most immediately popular work. It has remained in print ever since.

But we can pick almost any passage from the text and see how distinctive (and disorienting) it can be. Here are some lines following the governess' declaration that the children are lost and she can't save or shield them from corruption.

> It was a pity that, somehow, to settle this once for all, I had equally to re-enumerate the signs of subtlety that, in the afternoon, by the lake, had made a miracle of my show of self-possession. It was a pity to be obliged to re-investigate the certitude of the moment itself and repeat how it had come to me as a revelation that the inconceivable communion I then surprised must have been for both parties a matter of habit. It was a pity I should have had to quaver out again the reasons for my not having, in my delusion, so much as questioned that the little girl saw our visitant even as I actually saw Mrs. Grose herself, and that she wanted, by just so much as she did thus see, to make me suppose she did n't, and at the same time, without showing anything, arrive at a guess as to whether I myself did! It was a pity I needed to recapitulate the portentous little activities by which she sought to divert my attention—the imperceptible increase of movement, the greater intensity of play, the singing, the gabbling of nonsense and the invitation to romp. (*TotS* 8: 60–1)

It would be a pity to translate this into simpler language, plain syntax, and short sentences. Many portions of late James require rereading and some mental revisions. One could summarize James's long sentences and paragraphs but not without losing the compulsive flow, the fierce attempt on the narrator's part to seem in control of the situation and her thoughts, contradiction and overprecision. The repeated opening phrase (anaphora) and the leisurely parallel structure unify the passage but emphasizes the redundant (reinforced by the vocabulary: *reenumerate, reinvestigate, repeat, quaver out again, recapitulate*). The certainty is undercut by seeing and knowing what cannot be seen or known: *inconceivable communion, imperceptible increase*. Words like *miracle, certitude*, and *revelation* seem at odds with *having to quaver, my delusion*, and then the central contradiction: "she wanted, by just so much as she did thus see, to make me suppose she did n't. . . ." Every sentence is interrupted by a number of interpolated phrases that make it difficult to read aloud. It is interesting to note that the late style was simultaneous with James's switch to dictation; some have speculated this caused James to simplify or remove extraneous punctuation because every punctuation mark had to be stipulated for the typist.

Let us consider another, shorter passage when the governess has gone from thinking of the children as angels to perceiving them as "little wretches" colluding with "the others."

> After these secret scenes I chattered more than ever, going on volubly enough till one of our prodigious hushes occurred—I can call them nothing else—the strange dizzy lift or swim (I try for terms!) into a stillness, a pause of all life, that had nothing to do with the more or less noise we at the moment might be engaged in making and that I could hear through any intensified mirth or quickened recitation or louder strum of the piano. (*TotS* 13: 81)

This is just a single sentence, 80 words and with a minimum of punctuation. This causes us to speed along reflecting the narrator's voluble chatter. While we can see some of the same characteristics evident in the first passage, the first uses many abstract words of a higher register; the words here are all simple and more generally monosyllabic. Both are about the narrator's awareness of the inadequacy of language to convey her experiences and beliefs (in the first case to Mrs. Grose and in the second case to whoever she thinks of as the future readers of her manuscript). "I can call them nothing else—the strange dizzy lift or swim (I try for terms!)." What is a "prodigious hush"? The passage alternates between silences (*stillness, pause of all life, more or less noise*) and sounds (*chattered, recitation, louder strum of the piano*). The voluble chatter or "intensified mirth" is hollow, joyless, and forced. Mary Cross sees Henry James's style as "proto-deconstruction." "His syntax does something to words, opening them up, stretching their possibilities and trope-ing them in the torque of his sentences in his effort to include '*all* the dimensions' and to control the text. . . . Qualifying to the point of seeming surreal, James's sentences end up pushing meaning just out of reach, beyond themselves, in a dynamic of continuous change and supplement" (Cross 1993: 3). More recently, Kevin Ohi notes that "James's writing continually throws a reader off balance with disorienting mixings of register and sudden shifts of tone, with unexpected syntactical inversions and equivocal reifications that hover at indeterminate levels of abstraction, with pronouns that divide their allegiances between any number of more or less distant antecedents, with symbolic and figural language that spurns subservience, determining plots and becoming visible on depicted landscapes, and with coercively authoritative voices that unexpectedly cede their perspective or suddenly give way to ironical deflation" (Ohi 2006: 140).

What we find here in just these two brief passages is typical of James's late style. Most obvious is perhaps repetition, but repetition with variation that does not settle meaning. Sheila Teahan, for example, has analyzed the governess' "use of the word 'literally' in contexts that call attention to themselves as incongruous and counterintuitive" (Teahan 2006: 63). Teahan provides a close reading of the 15 times it is used in the work, never following its normative sense of actually or really. She also analyzes the repeated metaphorical use of *tracing* and *sketching* (Teahan 2006: 70–3). About whatever occurred to cause Miles' expulsion turns on the word *obscurity*: "deep obscurity continued to cover the region of the boy's conduct at school" (*TotS* 4: 43) becomes "the hideous obscure" that the governess dare not plunge into toward the end of the work (*TotS* 22: 112). Sometimes the repetition is of a rare word that seems out of place for the young governess (such as the term she employs for "give up," *abjure*).

> To gaze into the depths of blue of the child's eyes and pronounce their loveliness a trick of premature cunning was to be guilty of a cynicism in preference to which I naturally preferred to abjure my judgement and, so far as might be, my agitation. I could n't abjure for merely wanting to, but I could repeat to Mrs. Grose—as I did there, over and over, in the small hours—. . . (*TotS* 8: 60)

Silence, and attempts to say the unsayable, as well as breaks and gaps, as well as fragmentary dialogue completed by others, make language sometime into a game of interrogation as well as interpretation, of coercion of the reader as well as of characters. When the governess asks Mrs. Grose about whether she has "never known him to be bad," Mrs. Grose replies, "Oh never known him—I don't pretend *that*!"

> I was upset again. "Then you *have* known him—?"
> "Yes, indeed, Miss, thank God!"
> On reflexion I accepted this. "You mean that a boy who never is—?"
> "Is no boy for *me*!"
> [The next day she asks Mrs. Grose about the previous governess and is told Miss Jessel was almost as young and pretty as the narrator.]

"He seems to like us young and pretty!"

"Oh he *did*," Mrs. Grose assented: it was the way he liked every one!" She had no sooner spoken indeed than she caught herself up. "I mean that's *his* way—he master's."

I was struck. "But of whom did you speak first?"

She looked blank, but she coloured. "Why of *him*."

"Of the master?"

"Of who else?"

There was so obviously no one else that the next moment I had lost my impression of her having accidentally said more than she meant. (*TotS* 2: 35)

What is the effect of these elements? How does such stylistic indirection function in the text? William Veeder argues that James's additional clauses, interpolating metaphor, and negative elements in what would otherwise be straightforward, unproblematic sentences, creates mystery.

> The very presence of an initial metaphor of negation will impel us farther into the passage for elucidation. . . . We escape our initial puzzlement only by joining the metaphoric and literal or negative and positive elements together in our minds. Our minds are made to move, to jump like a spark across a dark gap. We ourselves create that relationship, that connection, which is meaning. (Veeder 1975: 214)

Many of James's critics in the mid-twentieth century understood James's tight and twisting style as an emotionally distancing technique for the intensely private James. They relate his seeming textual hesitations and unsolved mysteries to his guarded writing even in his correspondence (this was before the most passionate and seemingly homoerotic letters were made available to scholars), and to his requests to correspondents to burn any of his letters in their possession. It went along with his unknown sexual experiences, his unrepentant bachelorhood, and the two main images he left. There is first mystique and reverence of "the Master" for other writers (Joseph Conrad, Stephen Crane, Ford Madox Ford in the beginning to century, Cynthia Ozick, Joyce Carol Oates, and others in the 1960s). Then there is the pompous and stiff figure of parody and cartoons (both of these images conveniently gathered in Adeline Tintner's brilliant *Henry James's Legacy* [1998]). It has become increasingly commonplace to connect James's oblique and complex later style with his emotional and repressed or occluded homoerotic or homosexual life (see, for example, Ohi 2007: 126–7). Ohi argues that it is here that evidence of the "queerness of James's writings" can be found, rather than in "its representation of marginal sexualities" (Ohi 2006: 141).

GENRE

Genres are shared classifications of texts used loosely by readers, publishers, and authors. To call *The Turn of the Screw* a ghost story, immediately draws attention to how it is different from most other ghost stories, including other James's approximately twenty stories in this genre. It is far more of a contemporary, realistic text than other Victorian ghost stories (think of Dickens's *Christmas Carol*) because so much remains unknown and unsaid, in particular the "reality" of the ghosts (we will discuss this in Chapter 3). It was a popular and recognized genre in the magazines of the day and when asked by an editor to provide a Christmas-time ghost story, James returned to an anecdote he had heard at the Archbishop of Canterbury's dinner table two years earlier. As artful as the story might be, James treated it as trivial, as "essentially a pot-boiler and a *jeu d'esprit*" (in a letter to author H. G. Wells). To Frederic W. H. Myers of the Society for Psychical Research, James wrote, "The *T. of the S.* is a very mechanical matter, I honestly think—an inferior, a merely *pictorial*, subject and rather a shameless pot-boiler" (*TotS* 177–8). In his 1908 preface to the volume of the New York Edition that included *The Turn of the Screw*, it seems like James was happy to sow genre-confusion.

James begins with the "real-life" discussion that is reminiscent of frame setting of his work. The talk had turned "to apparitions and night fears, to the marked and sad drop in the general supply, and still more in the general commodities."

The good, the really effective and heart-shaking, ghost-stories (roughly so to term them) appeared all to have been told, and neither new crop nor new type in any quarter awaited us. The new type indeed, the mere modern "psychical" case, washed clean of all queerness as by exposure to a flowing laboratory tap, and equipped with credentials vouching for this—the new type clearly promised little, for the more it was respectably certified the less it seemed of a nature to rouse the dear old sacred terror. (*TotS* 180)

James then suggests that his work is "a fairy tale, pure and simple," a game, an exercise, an improvisation, an "excursion into chaos," a "piece of ingenuity . . . of cold artistic calculation, an *amusette* to catch those not easily caught . . ., the jaded, the disillusioned, the fastidious" (*TotS* 181, 182). Ghosts, such as those of the traditional ghost story or those antiseptic case histories of the SPR or journals such as *Borderland*, cannot achieve "the dreadful, my designed horror. Good ghosts . . . make poor subjects, and it was clear from the first my hovering prowling blighting presences, my pair of abnormal agents, would have to depart from the rules." Peter Quint and Miss Jessel are not so much ghosts, "but goblins, elves, imps, demons . . ." (*TotS* 184).

James's work, then, is both a ghost story that fit the expectations of the editor of *Collier's Weekly* and the many readers who were part of that Victorian tradition and a departure from the norm "to catch those not easily caught." A large and convincing body of critical writing patiently finds models for *The Turn of the Screw* in the hundreds of "psychical cases" documented or refuted in the SPR reports (Banta 1972; Beidler 1989; Lustig 1994; Sheppard 1974). These works also document the widespread interest in the late nineteenth century in the supernatural and psychic phenomenon (telepathy, mediums, automatic writing, séances, etc.). Fascination with the supernatural cut across all social classes and educational backgrounds (as illustrated by William and Henry James). The ghost tradition in literature can be traced by to ancient Greek epic and tragedy, through Shakespeare's *Hamlet* or *Macbeth* to mix with the Gothic in eighteenth and nineteenth centuries (interwoven with other genres through the works of Horace Walpole, Ann Radcliffe, Mary Shelley, Dickens, and Wilkie Collins, and the Brontës). In the decade preceding *The Turn of the Screw*, we can also immediately call to mind the success of such works as Robert Louis Stevenson's *Dr. Jekyll and Mr. Hyde* (1886), Oscar Wilde's *The Picture of Dorian Gray* (1890), or Bram Stoker's *Dracula* (1897). The isolated setting of Bly, the luxury and emptiness of the estate, the innocents endangered by supernatural forces, the young woman imperilled and without any male support, secrets about death and hints of sexual transgression all immediately point to the Gothic tradition. In addition to the ghostly and the Gothic, there are powerful echoes of fairy tales such as "Hansel and Gretel," "Cinderella," and "Bluebeard" (see the essays by Lisa G. Chinitz 1994, Christine Butterworth-McDermott 2007, and Victoria Coulson 2007, esp. 180–4).

It is not only that the author and readers of *The Turn of the Screw* are aware of these intertexts, but so is the main narrator. During the governess' first tour of Bly, she is struck by Flora's "confidence and courage" as the little girl leads her through "empty chambers and dull corridors, on crooked staircases that made me pause and even on the summit of an old machicolated square tower that made me dizzy . . . I had the view of a castle of romance inhabited by a rosy sprite, such a place as would somehow . . . take call colour out of story-books and fairy-tales. Was n't it just a story-book over which I had fallen a-doze and a-dream?" (*TotS* 1: 32–3). After her first vision of a male figure in the battlements, she wonders, "Was there a 'secret' at Bly—a mystery of Udolpho or an insane, an unmentionable relative kept in unsuspected confinement?" (*TotS* 4: 41), alluding to both Ann Radcliffe's novel *The Mysteries of Udolpho* (1794) and to Charlotte Brontë's *Jane Eyre* (1847) (another text of a governess trying to read the secrets of the extraordinary master and children). We might also see that she has expectations on taking the position of a fairy-tale ending, a living-happily-every-after epilogue.

STRUCTURE AND NARRATIVE

The mid-century Victorian novel of Charles Dickens, William Thackeray, Benjamin Disraeli, Anthony Trollope, Mrs. Gaskell, and the Brontës was discursive and often digressive, perhaps because they were almost always first serialized before being published in book form. Serial publication allowed for broadly drawn characters whether comical or evil for aiding the readers' memories when weeks or months might pass between appearances of the characters. It allowed for subplots and different moods to appear in each section published in the journal. The aesthetic norm was to have strong closure, displaying poetic justice, and often an epigraph indicating what "happens" with all of the characters *after* the end of the plot. The reader was not allowed to stray from a predetermined interpretation: there were prefatory comments by an omniscient narrator who would appear periodically to make sure the reader was understanding the moral or social message at each juncture. This was the form of the popular novel; it is unlike *The Turn of the Screw* in every way.

The other influential model for James's fiction was from Realism. These authors (such as Thomas Hardy) wanted to avoid the artificiality of closure or the predictable form; they wanted clear and graphic descriptions of what is really found in everyday life, and a removal of unlikely coincidence and, perhaps especially, poetic justice (which was self-evidently rare in the "real world"), which required that the good would be rewarded and the bad punished in proportion to their acts. Naturalism added the element of determinism to Realism, treating the novel more like sociological documents. Naturalists posited that if a character of a certain social class and occupation finds him or herself in this particular situation at this moment, this is what is bound to happen. James's stylistic density or indirection works against the goals of Realism or Naturalism; there the language is meant to be a transparent medium, always working to advance the illusion of presenting the "real," to be mimetic. It has recently been argued that James's late style is antimimetic and throws off the Victorian novel's concentration on the plot and determinative structure and closure. According to Kevin Ohi, "James disrupts the possibility of conceiving of novelistic language in mimetic terms; his late style—not only its famous density and obscurity of reference, but also its characteristic disorientations of intelligibility, from its sudden alternations of tone and voice to its mixing of linguistic registers in favored tropes such as syllepsis or zeugma to its unevenly ironized and ironizing narrative perspectives—puts into practice this anti-mimetic theory" (Ohi 2007: 128).

We started this chapter by saying that no other authors could be mistaken for James. A turn on this would be to note that all of James's narrators, whatever their backgrounds, social status, genders, or nationalities sound like James and like each other (contrast this with the works of Dickens and Hardy among the Victorians or James Joyce or William Faulkner as examples of modernists for whom style varies constantly, especially to reflect different narrative voices within the same works). In this way, James resembles more closely more hermetic modernist experimental writers such as Gertrude Stein, Samuel Beckett, or Wallace Stevens. David Kurnick, considering the characteristic "mannerisms" of James's "late style" in an analysis of *The Wings of the Dove*, notes "The speakers, addressees, and subjects are distributed over the entire social landscape of the book. But these quite different characters address each other in almost indistinguishable patterns." Although James's purported aesthetic for the novel is for individual centers of consciousness, this is counteracted by the uniformity of style, "inundating the drama of moral and perspectival difference in a bath of stylistic indistinction" (Kurnick 2007: 215, 216). This also works against the mimetic surface of the text.

The Turn of the Screw appeared in a number of ways during James's lifetime and this has an impact on both the writing and the reading. The first publication was in installments in *Collier's Weekly* from January 27–April 16, 1898. There is not as much control by the author of the textual environment with the serial format as in a single book publication (of course, the extratextual environment in which real readers through time or in different places and circumstances read the work is entirely outside of authorial control). The twelve installments, spread through four months, competed for the reader's continued attention and memory of previous episodes (as well as the reader's nonreading life while newspaper headlines included multiple wars and the usual array of crimes, scandals). Every issue had other stories in various stages of serialization, along with advertisements, essays, and other elements. Chief among these distractions, as far as James was concerned, was the illustrations commissioned by the editors (John La Farge created the picture of the governess with her arm around Miles that appeared at the start of every episode and Eric Pape provided illustrations for each published section). James was hostile toward illustrations for fiction because of the way it immediately limited the readers' imagination or the possible ambiguities or suspensions of certainties provided by the words (see Cappello 1992, esp. 157–60; Wendy Graham 2003; Sonstegard 2005). For example, Pape's illustrations show the apparitions as actually they are (since we are seeing in the third person, as it were, not through the governess' eyes, as in the text). For the frame narrator of *The Turn of the Screw*, the disappointing, incomplete last story of the evening was "like the mere opening of a serial" (*TotS* 25). After serialization, the story was published with "The Covering End," a minor work, a play recast into a short story, under the title *The Two Magics*. Ten years after the serial version, James revised the work and wrote a preface for it in a volume of his New York Edition, an ambitious selection of his lifework. This did not have illustrations other than photographs selected by James at the start of each volume.

The Turn of the Screw does not begin with the first-person narration of the governess. It has a frame story with a different unnamed first-person narrator describing a traditional Christmas eve swapping of ghost stories. The party group is not only aristocratic, while the actual readers were of course middle class, but critical; they judge the stories according to effectiveness and use the vocabulary of case histories. They stand in for the readers and instead of distancing bring the readers into the group gathered around the fireside. Their questions might be the readers' questions. They are tantalized by what Douglas reveals about the story concerning two children, a story that nothing touches "For dreadful—dreadfulness! . . . For general uncanny ugliness and horror and pain" (*TotS* 23). They want such a horrific story immediately but he cannot tell it from memory. He has kept the manuscript locked up for many years and it must be sent for, the reading put off. But this discursive space is used to give the background about the respectability and reliability of the governess ("the most agreeable woman I've ever known in her position; she'd have been worthy of any whatever"), as well as expository information about her unworldly background and the uncle in Harley Street. It also explains how the uncle had set everything up at Bly, designed to keep Flora and Miles at a distance and the extraordinary requirement that she should not contact him about anything (26–8). The narrator of the frame is viewed by Douglas as especially perceptive; just before Douglas dies he passes the manuscript on to the narrator who now is sharing it with the readers. Love is involved but the governess' text will not reveal her love "in any literal vulgar way" (25). The narrator thinks it was better that some ladies "thank heaven," departed; they represented the vulgar reader. "But that only made his little final auditory more compact and select, kept it, round the hearth, subject to a common thrill" (26). The frame is important in setting readers up for certain sorts of interpretations.

We don't realize until after we have finished reading the entire work that this is just a partial frame. We could contrast it with a similar frame device used by Joseph Conrad in *Heart of Darkness* (published in 1899, the year after James's work). There the frame narrator is one of a five friends on the deck of ship in the Thames; the group is identified only by their occupations. As sunset approaches, Marlow suddenly launches into speech and "we knew we were fated . . . to hear about one of Marlow's inconclusive experiences." Marlow's story goes back in time to Roman Britain, it travels to Brussels and the

Congo. But it moves a number of times from Marlow's first-person narration to the frame narrator who observes what is happening at the present moment. After the end of Marlow's long and painful reminiscence, it returns to the group on the Thames as the director notes they have lost the ebb of the tide and there is a final reflection by the frame narrator about the story Marlow has just conveyed. That return is surprisingly missing from *The Turn of the Screw*. Douglas presents the governess' manuscript (now in the possession of the frame narrator so we do not have any doubt about its absolute fidelity) without any interruptions or questions from the listeners. The last paragraph ends the governess' story with the death of Miles; there is no further statement from Douglas about what happened to the governess or the other characters afterward, no symmetrical return to the original frame.

When the frame ends, we not only shift to a new first-person narrator, but this change entails social class and gender. It is unusual for James to use first person in his fiction but this is a sort of comical ventriloquism: a male character reading a manuscript written by a female character in a text by a male author using a female persona. One reason for James not to have used his customary omniscient third-person narrator is because of the question of reliability that can be opened. While the omniscient narrator is presumptively reliable, all first-person narrators must develop and sustain the readers' trust in their representation of events or their interpretations of the other characters. We should keep in mind that all first-person narrators are unreliable to widely varying degrees (including the writers of letters, autobiographies, or Author's Prefaces). Since the issue of ambiguity is the main focus of *Turn of the Screw* criticism, we will take that up in Chapter 3.

The governess' narrative is sharply circumscribed. Except for a brief opening describing her only meeting with the uncle in Harley Street when he hires her, the rest of the work takes place in the confines of Bly, its grounds and eccentric architecture. Letters arrive occasionally at Bly, but they do not get sent out. We have only a handful of characters: the governess, the uncle, Miles and Flora, Miss Jessel and Peter Quint, and Mrs. Grose (the other servants at Bly or the masters at Miles's school are alluded to but make no appearances). The time frame is brief: five months, from June through November. Even the governess' sightings of the "spirits" are rare for a ghost story (just four visits for each, clustered in the Summer and in November). The drive of the story is progressively toward the final moment, very much along the lines of the classic tragic plot (and unlike James's other plots). The young governess is first immediately overwhelmed by the beauty and goodness of the children and the good fortune of having her position at Bly, and the floating possibility of pleasing her remote employer by showing her command. After her first apperception of a figure that she understands is the spirit of the dead Peter Quint (after piecing together fragments from the reluctant Mrs. Grose), she first thinks that the children are in danger and she is the only one who can screen them from harm. Soon she thinks it is too late; the children are already lost and she must take steps to expel the corrupt forces of the dead servant and dead governess working through the children. She makes Mrs. Grose flee Bly with Flora so the governess can force a confession from Miles which will somehow purify him. She wants him to declare that he sees Peter Quint as she does and Miles, his heart failing, dies in her arms: "We were alone with the quiet day, and his little heart, dispossessed, had stopped" (*TotS* 24: 120). This is the tragic ending rather than the fairy tale or saved maiden conclusion the genre hints might have led us to expect. One has to go to Thomas Hardy's blighted families and indifferent universe in *Tess of the D'Urbervilles* or *Jude the Obscure* for something comparable.

QUESTIONS

1. Would you say the Author's Preface and the partial frame clarifies or complicates the understanding of *The Turn of the Screw*? What are your reasons?
2. Select a long paragraph or a page of *The Turn of the Screw* you feel exemplifies James's later style and analyze its features. What are the advantages of creating a form of writing that resists immediate comprehension?
3. Of the many genres critics have found within *Turn of the Screw*, which do you find most applicable? Are genre classifications useful or do they prevent possible interpretations?

CHAPTER 3

READING *THE TURN OF THE SCREW*

AMBIGUITY AND THE READER

Despite the assertion by the governess halfway through her narrative that "There was no ambiguity in anything" (*TotS* 6: 54), readers find ambiguity throughout this text. Although the action of the story is focused and restricted, it is filled with unresolved questions, mysteries that are raised and lost, concerning matters profound and trivial. Since the sole source of information is the governess, there are no outside sources (either the summarizing or commenting third-person omniscient narrator or competing or confirming first-person narrators) to help point to the truthfulness or facts or lack of these in the governess' manuscript. Since we have no return to the outside frame, we do not know what the reaction of the frame narrator was or whether any questions were then asked of Douglas about what happened with the governess and Flora immediately after the death of Miles (for that matter, what brought Douglas's family to hire the governess after her fiasco at her first job? It's difficult to picture the uncle's letter of recommendation).

We mentioned in Chapter 2 James's devices of indirection and narrative gaps that are common through his late style. The governess rides an emotional roller-coaster of too much certainty and self-confidence followed by too much doubt, of romanticizing and idealizing Bly and the children and then seeing the place as cursed and the children as corrupted and evil. This is signaled in the first sentence of governess' narration: "I remember the whole beginning as a succession of flights and drops, a little see-saw of the right throbs and the wrong" (*TotS* 1: 29). She is giddy with her good fortune at being at such a place with such beautiful, well-behaved children, imbued with self-importance by the special demand by her employer not to contact him about anything and to solve all questions herself, and both excited and brought to nervous exhaustion by her battle to protect the children from evil.

Suspense surrounds Miles's dismissal from school, the first crisis in the governess' career. The reader never learns what the letter from the school actually says; the governess hands it to Mrs. Grose to read and then we find the housekeeper is illiterate. The governess is about to read it to her but does not. Instead she summarizes and then makes an unspoken leap of inference: "They go into no particulars. They simply express their regret that it should be impossible to keep him. That can have but one meaning." (*TotS* 2: 33–4). Mrs. Grose might be blank but the readers (particularly in the period immediately following the Oscar Wilde scandal) might think of other possible meanings before the governess asserts, after a break of four lines, the unspoken words from the masters are that Miles is "an injury to others." She doesn't ask Miles directly but he has convinced her by his goodness there could be no truth to whatever it was "the stupid sordid head-masters" vindictively charged. She keeps twisting the gaps of the letter; nearly sixty pages later, when Mrs. Grose declares they have never known the least reason for Miles's expulsion, the governess is much more explicit. He was expelled for "wickedness. For what else—when he's so clever and beautiful and perfect? Is he stupid? Is he untidy? Is he infirm? Is he ill-natured? He's exquisite—so it can only be *that*; and that would open up the whole thing" (*TotS* 16: 91). Later Mrs. Grose offers another theory: "He stole letters!" (*TotS* 21: 109).

In the closing pages, the governess is intent on making Miles reveal the nature of his transgression at school and when he finally does, it is more evocative than clear: he "said things" to those he liked. Whatever words he shared "they must have repeated them. To those *they* liked" (*TotS* 24: 118–19). Whatever those words were, they were "too bad" for the masters to have written in the letter announcing his expulsion. The confession remains unsatisfactory and obscure for the governess; she rejects it with low force: "Stuff and nonsense! . . . What *were* those things?" The interrogation is interrupted by the governess seeing Peter Quint and Miles's sudden death. What were the words that were so transgressive? If ten readers were assigned to write down the suppressed words, there would be ten different plausible responses. There is also the possibility that there may be some other reasons for Miles's expulsion that he is unwilling to say to the governess but under duress he supplies something relatively innocuous (and perhaps that is what the governess feels when she rejects Miles's answers).

Because the story stops exactly as Miles's "little heart, dispossessed, had stopped," we never know what the governess feels at that time or years after when she decided to write the manuscript. Did she feel horror with having seemingly driven Miles to his death or does she feel triumphant at having driven the corruption from Miles, at having restored him to childhood purity even if that was at the cost of his life? Did her understanding of what occurred at Bly change through time? What finally prompted her to write down the experience and then to be sure to entrust it to a sympathetic reader, Douglas? The only emotion the governess explicitly feels in the moment before Miles's death is *pride*. As to what she feels a moment later when she realizes the boy she holds is dead, that is left to the reader to fill in: "I held him—it may be imagined with what a passion; but at the end of a minute I began to feel what it truly was that I held" (*TotS* 24: 120).

There are questions left in the air about the lives and deaths of Miss Jessel and Peter Quint. How did the Miss Jessel die? How long after her leaving Bly did her death occur and was there anything sinister about it? About what exactly was she not careful? The sole source of information on these issues for the governess, and so for the reader, is Mrs. Grose, whose constant equivocations about the former governess and valet. Both Mrs. Grose and the governess avoid any overt mention of the sexual and so their dialogue is a play of omission and self-censorship.

> I had a scruple, but I overcame it. "Was she careful—particular?"
>
> Mrs. Grose appeared to try to be conscientious. "About some things—yes."
>
> "But not about all?"
>
> Again she considered. "Well, Miss—she's gone. I won't tell tales."
>
> "I quite understand your feeling," I hastened to reply; but I thought it after an instant not opposed to this concession to pursue: "Did she die here?"
>
> "No—she went off."
>
> I don't know what there was in the brevity of Mrs. Grose's that struck me as ambiguous. "Went off to die?" Mrs. Grose looked

straight out of the window. . . . "She was taken ill, you mean, and went home?"

"She was not taken ill, so far as appeared, in this house. She left it, at the end of the year, to go home. . . . But our young lady never came back. . . . I heard from the master that she was dead."

I turned this over. "But of what?"

"He never told me!" (*TotS* 2: 36)

The governess' interpretation of Mrs. Grose's attempts (and failures) to be clear and truthful occur again and again: "appeared to try to be conscientious." What are the tales she won't tell? It is widely treated as a certainty by critics that Miss Jessel was pregnant with Quint's child when she left and that she died in childbirth, but those suppositions are entirely without textual foundations. Reading too much in the blank spaces of the text duplicates the way the governess' hermeneutic obsession leads to her certainties of the corruption of the children. Mrs. Grose's remarks about Quint are similarly vague. For example, were the details that came out at the inquest after his death? His death was accounted for by liquor and the icy path but there were "strange passages and perils, secret disorders, vices more than suspected, that would have accounted for a good deal more" (*TotS* 6: 52–3). We are left to wonder how, when alive, Quint and Miss Jessel exerted an evil influence over the children other than through the children's awareness of the couple's hinted sexual relationship.

The overwhelming ambiguity, one that underlies and drives not only the narrative but the majority of interpretations of the story, deals with the "reality" or "existence" of the ghostly. In other words, is the governess a reliable narrator? Does she "really see" the spirits or ghosts of the dead Miss Jessel and Peter Quint or are these hallucinations? We mentioned in Chapter 2 both the established genres (including the ghost story and the Gothic) and James's mixing of genres, as well as the widespread interest, both popular and pseudo-scientific, in the supernatural and in communicating with the dead. In the tradition of ghosts from the epic to folklore to literature, there is a wide range of representation of spirits in all cultures, but there are shared conventions, rules, and internal consistency within a work or time period. For example, ghosts appeared because they had messages or unfinished tasks or because they sought vengeance. Shakespeare's audience did not question whether the ghost of old King Hamlet was "real" and was briefly visiting Elsinore from Hell to tell Prince

Hamlet how he had been poisoned and that Hamlet needed to kill his uncle Claudius immediately. Multiple witnesses see the ghost and a scholar, Horatio, confirms the identity of the ghost (to be certain it is not a demon disguised as ghost). Similarly, audiences did not worry themselves over the "reality" of vampires in *Dracula* or the witches in *Macbeth* or the gods and goddesses interceding in human affairs in the ancient epic or tragedy. Certainly most of readers of *The Turn of the Screw*, when it first appeared and in the century since, similarly accept at face value the governess' account of the sightings of the spectral presences of the former servants (perhaps it is prejudging to call them ghosts).

But there is doubt sown with each reported appearance. It is not merely because no one else in the story acknowledges seeing the ghosts even under strong interrogation by the governess. The ghost cases reported by the SPR have many instances where ghosts make their appearances known only to specific individuals and remain unnoticed by others (see the primary documents on ghosts sightings about the time of the publication of this work in *TotS* 144–71; also see the books Banta 1972; Beidler 1989; Lustig 1994; and Sheppard 1974: chapter 8). When the governess sees the figure in the tower she later identifies as Quint, she has just been enjoying a recurring romantic fantasy: "it would be as charming as a charming story suddenly to meet some one. Some one would appear there at the turn of a path and would stand before me and smile and approve. . . . I only asked that he should *know*; and the only way to be, and the kind light of it, in his handsome face . . ." (*TotS* 3: 39). The handsome, approving vision that has cheered her first weeks at Bly is of course of the wealthy master in Harley Street; in fulfilling the special trust he has placed in the young governess has given her such pleasure, such a sense of worth and power (38–9). Then the handsome face in her imagination is replaced by the surprising and "violent perception" that "the man who met my eyes was not the person I had precipitately supposed. There came to me thus a bewilderment of vision." Despite this "bewilderment of vision" and her shock, the governess repeats how accurate and definite her account is ("the man who looked at me over the battlements was as definite as a picture in a frame" [40], "I saw him as I see the letters I form on this page" [41]). This encounter is a visual showdown, a "straight mutual stare," intense fixed gazes until the man turns away. There is a gap of time; for awhile, the governess stays where she was during this initial contest of wills, which she characterizes as "collision." She is turning over the sight of the man with a "confusion of curiosity and dread." In her agitation, she somehow wanders around the grounds of Bly covering 3 miles and it is dark before she finally goes back inside the house. Her encounter with the man is sandwiched between her happy romantic daydreaming and a jump to the possibility that Bly held dark secrets as in Charlotte Brontë's *Jane Eyre* (with the mysterious master with his strict and strange conditions for her work as Rochester, with the governess as the intelligent heroine; on the many parallels between *Turn of the Screw* and *Jane Eyre* see Bell 1993: 99–104; Kauffman 1986: 210–17). Oddly, she didn't rush inside the house to seek safety but remains alone outside after the encounter, and her first decision is to keep the encounter from Mrs. Grose.

Through the next encounter, on a rainy Sunday, she has gone alone into the dining room and sees the man outside pressing his face against the window staring at her again as if they were far closer mentally as well as physically. "He appeared . . . with a nearness that represented a forward stride in our intercourse and made me, as I met him, catch my breath and turn cold. . . . it was as if I had been look-ing at him for years and known him always" (*TotS* 4: 44). She has a "shock of certitude," a "flash of knowledge," that the man had come there looking for someone else; this fills her with "a sudden vibration of duty and courage" (45). The appearance of Quint at the window is repeated in his last encounter with the governess (24: 116–17). Whether she thinks this man is a trespasser or something evil, her actions are again counterintuitive. She does not call out for help from Mrs. Grose and the other servants (always vaguely uncharacterized). Instead, she races around outside to the drive and the terrace, despite the rain, despite the fact the others are waiting for her to join them in going to church. The man is gone but she waits, standing on the lawn to give him time to return. The grounds in every direction "were empty with a great emptiness. . . . He was there or not there: not there if I didn't see him." Before finally giving up and going back inside the house, she impulsively goes to the dining hall window to stare inside, to look through the eyes of the man, as it were, to try to dis-cover what he had been able to see. The repetition is helped because by this time Mrs. Grose is in the room and jumps with fright on seeing the governess' face at the window. Even after frightening Mrs. Grose, the governess stays at the window and "thought of more things than one" without specifying anything. Although she portrays herself as deliberate and calmly analytical, she reveals her tendency to jump to interpretations without any solid information, to be reckless, and to want to draw herself close to the mysterious but exciting visitors, rather than to stay within the constraints of the mundane, well-lit, safe and predictable life of her occupation at the isolated estate.

The third encounter occurs in the middle of the night inside the house; the governess had been in bed reading a novel about a heroic but threatened woman (Henry Fielding's *Amelia* [1751]). Something she cannot identify drew her out to walk the dark house, feeling there was "something undefinably astir in the house" (*TotS* 9: 67). She sees Quint on the staircase and although he was "a living detestable presence," she felt no dread or terror until later. Importantly for her assertion of her sense of developing power over Quint, she declares Quint knew that she felt no terror before him: "I found myself at the end of an instant magnificently aware of this." She diminishes what should have been terrifying by standing her ground, staring back at Quint in silence until he turns his back and slinks off down the staircase into the darkness. She never again saw him in the house. But it is the end of her sleep; from then on, she stays awake as much as she can to be always on the lookout, leaving the room when she was sure Flora was asleep to patrol the halls and the staircase. Finally, after 11 nights, the governess sees not Quint but her predecessor, Miss Jessel, "her body half-bowed and her head, in an attitude of woe, in her hands" (*TotS* 10: 70). Readers not fully caught up in the reality of the ghosts might wonder about seeing this detail viewing in the dark staircase, the back of the melodramatically posed Miss Jessel (or the mental effects of 11 nights of little sleep and that frequently disturbed).

The first time the governess saw the apparition of Miss Jessel was in the middle of the day and on the periphery of a cheerful scene of happy play with Flora near the lake; the bright sunshine is part of the evidence to establish the reality of the ghosts. But then the governess begins to recognize the ghost prior to actually seeing her. She is certain she will see the dead governess even prior to using her physical senses, mentally predisposed for the other half of secret and disgraceful couple.

> I became aware . . . we had an interested spectator. . . . I began to take in with certitude and yet without direct vision the presence, a good way off, of a third person. . . . There was no ambiguity in

anything; none whatever at least in the conviction I from one moment to another found myself forming as to what I should see straight before me and across the lake as a consequence of raising my eyes. They were attached at this juncture to the stitching in which I was engaged, and I can feel once more the spasm of my effort not to move them till I should have so steadied myself as to be able to make up my mind what to do. There was an alien object in view—a figure whose right of presence I instantly and passionately questioned. (*TotS* 6: 54)

Though the two figures are equally ghostly or ghastly, equally evil or threatening, the governess does not experience the same sort of shock with Miss Jessel as she does with Quint. Even at a remove of years between the experience and the writing of her account, the governess can recount instants, moment-by-moment perception, extrasensual awareness, judgment, and certainty. Although assuring readers there is nothing at all ambiguous, nothing about the sightings of the apparitions proven; the evidence we might expect to be confirmed by the other residents of Bly remain solely the experience and testimony of the narrator.

Similarly, on the related issue of the children's awareness of the figures of Quint and Miss Jessel, and whether there is some continued influence by the dead servants on Miles and Flora, we can go only by the observations and certainties of the governess. After making a "positive identity of the apparition" of Miss Jessel at the lake, she watches Flora playing but the child gives no cries of alarm. The failure of the children to see what the governess sees, becomes the strongest proof for the governess that the children are complicit with the ghosts. Their happy playing, good behavior, and politeness, and their interest in the classroom activities, becomes the governess' paradoxical proof that they are lost to evil forces, that they are corrupted and somehow under the sway of the dead servants. The governess' logic here is that if they were not corrupted they would freely admit seeing what to her is clear and apparent. She forces this theory onto Mrs. Grose who also never sees the figures: "They *know*—it's too monstrous; they know, they know!"

"Two hours ago, in the garden . . . Flora *saw*!"
Mrs. Grose took it as she might have taken a blow in the stomach. "She has told you?" she panted.

"Not a word—that's the horror. She kept it to herself! The child of eight, *that* child!" Unutterable still for me was the stupefaction of it.

Mrs. Grose could only gape the wider. "Then how do you know?"

"I was there—I saw with my eyes: saw she was perfectly aware." (*TotS* 7: 56)

This assertion by the governess, that the children are purposely hiding from her their awareness of the presence of the ghosts, occurs with increasing frequency from this point on (see 10: 69–71; 13: 78–9). She sees the children as mocking her, intentionally distracting her from the question of the ghosts and their influence by their own feigned overwhelming goodness and beauty (see, for example, 9: 64–6). Since these are subtle turns, hard to articulate for the reader of her story, she keeps rejecting the idea that she is in any way subject to delusions. She is aggravated for a month by "the small ironic consciousness on the part of my pupils. It was not, I am as sure to-day as I was sure then, my mere infernal imagination" (13: 78). She imagines them enjoying coded messages to lead their guardian into "forbidden ground," such as the "question of the return of the dead in general" or about the late servants. She thinks of one using a "small, invisible nudge" on the other as they get advantage again and again of the governess (79). After such suspicions, she acknowledges that whether the children knew or had seen the ghosts had not been proven, and she speaks of her own "obsession" (80). She imagines forcing them to admit their collusion with the ghosts and that she would exalt, "'They're here, they're here, you little wretches . . ., and you can't deny it now!'"

What is most frightening to the governess is not the existence of the ghosts or any possible harm they might be able to do to her, but "the cruel idea that, whatever I had seen Miles and Flora saw *more*— things terrible and unguessable and that sprang from dreadful passages of intercourse in the past." Of course, what these terrible things are must remain unexpressed in the governess' manuscript; they are unspeakable. With the word "unguessable," she raises the idea that this secret knowledge is entirely beyond her limited exposure to such profane elements of the world (even years after the events at Bly when she writes the text). She cannot offer the reader anything concrete to flesh out, so to speak, this tantalizing hint. Her reticence here, as with her earlier gaps and hesitations, leaves the reader with a range of possibilities (different for different readers and necessarily outside of what might be available to the narrator). It is of a piece with whatever was behind Miles's expulsion from school or what was learned at Quint's inquest.

There are other unresolved questions regarding the motives for the narration, the intentions and audience for the governess in setting down these events years later, preserving them, and transmitting them (and then how she decided on entrusting Douglas and for what purpose, and then the frame narrator's motives). Neill Matheson has argued that the purposeful ambiguity and indirection are not the medium for the story, but they are the central site for James's sexual psychomachia. Matheson claims that

> James's erotic figurative language . . . is not simply a way of repre-senting sexual transgression; it is itself a transgressive perfor-mance, an instance of what [Eve Kosofsky] Sedgwick has called "queer performativity." His strangely equivocal figures, both ambiguous and arresting, are the very site of perverse erotic mean-ing in the story. (1999: 714)

Taking a completely different tack, focused on the narrator and staying within the bounds of the text, Marilyn C. Wesley reads *The Turn of the Screw* through memory and narrative theory derived from cognitive science. The moment at the end of the story, the death of Miles, is the most significant place in the governess' memory:

> [F]or the narrator, it signals her inadequacy as a competent governess. . . . Self-doubt, realized as a 'succession of flights and drops' of emotion . . ., shapes the entire narrative. And the vacilla-tion of confidence is also witnessed throughout by the governess's on-again off-again projection of the ghosts as a sign of her own failing, a pattern exaggerated by the sporadic visibility of Quint in the ultimate chapter. (Wesley 2004: 88)

This failure is also a collapse of her self-narrative (the projection of what she would do, how she expected her life to develop) and her identity (since that is unified with her new function as shown by her namelessness, that she can only be called "the governess"). According-ing to Wesley, "the abiding project of the governess's life has been the narration of the momentous memory of the death of little Miles as a means of redefining selfhood in the face of her early, painful failure to realize a new identity" (89).

READING THE MINDS: CONSCIOUSNESS, UNCONSCIOUSNESS, CHILDHOOD

Ambiguity has been a frustration for many readers of *The Turn of the Screw* (or many other modernist works), who want to supply a definitive answer to each of the questions we have raised in the first part of this chapter. This has, through most of the criticism written during the first 80 years after the work's first appearance, tended toward a binarism. The first group of readings argue the story can be taken "literally," as a straightforward Victorian ghost story about children corrupted by the transgressive relationships and sexual knowledge (however this might be understood to be transmitted to them) of the spirits of the dead servants; the children and ghosts are the focus. This approach is still probably the predominant mode for reading the story for those coming to it outside of the classroom or scholarly journal. The second mode in this binary path is to see the ghosts as hysterical projections from the disturbed mind of the narrator and so the children are victims; here the focus is on the unconscious mind of the governess and uses the tools of psychoanalysis (first following the work of Freud). In her recent survey of Jamesian psychoanalytic criticism, Julie Rivkin notes that, "Narrative, reading, representation, knowledge, secrecy, the uncanny, gender, sexuality, repression, the family, loss, identification, desire, transference—the list of psychoanalytic topics in James studies is not easily exhausted" (Rivkin 2007: 59). Beginning in the 1970s, with feminist studies and deconstruction, then more recently with gender studies, the earlier binarism has been broken in many different ways but may be summarized as feeling that there is much lost and nothing gained by simplifying and disambiguating James's work.

The governess' exaggerated fears concerning the secret adult knowledge passed to the children mirrors generally held *fin-de-siècle* fears of sexuality and lost innocence (just as works such as Stevenson's *Dr. Jekyll and Mr. Hyde*, Conrad's *Heart of Darkness*, H. G. Wells's *The Time Machine*, or, for that matter, Freud's *The Interpretation of Dreams*, reflect Victorian post-Darwinian anxieties about degeneration and the permanent savage hidden just below the surface of the "civilized" urban-dweller). Children in Victorian fiction are often endangered by their parents' financial miscalculations and entailed wills, pressures to marry only the potential spouse the parent has selected, almost always for reasons of money or social connections. They are subject to the parents' obsessions and eccentricities, life-changing scandals, early deaths, being orphaned and sent to night-marish relatives, prison-like schools, or to unpleasant work, the girls often working as governesses. Outside of the world of the novel, and increasingly, at the end of the century even within fiction of the Naturalists and Realists, there were the dangers of crime, prostitution, terrible poverty, and sexual assault and illegitimacy. In James's fiction that focuses on children, the parents are derelict or negligent in their role as guides and protectors (see "The Pupil," "The Author of Beltraffio," *What Maisie Knew*, and *The Awkward Age*). Maeve Pearson argues that in James's work,

> the nursery harbors its own domestic and private dangers . . . (rep-resented . . . by the broader underlying theme of parental neglect or abandonment in all of these stories . . . or that circle around 'genteel' servants (tutors, manservants, and governesses). The resultant vortices of adult passions that James's children get caught up in transform the sanctuary of the nursery into a claus-trophobic and imprisoning space. (2007: 107–8)

All of the adults in *The Turn of the Screw* are variously incapable. The titles turn out to be ironic: master, governess, schoolmasters. The master of Bly is never in residence and has created as his most impor-tant concern absolute ignorance about his charges; suddenly made the guardian of two young children was difficult for "a lone man without the right sort of experience or a grain of patience" (*TotS* 27). He left his niece and nephew in the hands of servants who are obvi-ously unsuited for their work, especially without the slightest super-vision, first Miss Jessel and his former valet, Peter Quint (although he must be aware of the unsavoury problems revealed at Quint's inquest), and then Mrs. Grose and the governess who were placed "in supreme authority." The master's wilful ignorance, his lack of due diligence, shows his lack of mastery. Despite the implications of her title, the governess cannot control her actions, her imagination, her fears, or her students. In the frame narration we learn the governess was only 20 years old during the time of her adventure at Bly and this was the first time she had worked in a classroom (which may be why almost no scenes of teaching are depicted except for a geography name-game by the lake and some mention of French and recitation from memory). As Marilyn C. Wesley has argued, "A significant 'turn of the screw' in James's novella is the escalating abdication of social responsibility that culminates in Miles's death. . . . The ghosts in this story signify the narrator's lapses of confidence because they are the representations of absence: dead and dishonoured, Jessel and Quint, are the negative signs of failed community" (Wesley 2004: 92). Looking at the work from a completely different perspective, as a "homospectral" story, John Fletcher notes:

> The precondition for the events at Bly, both those of the past as well as those of the narrative's present, is one that *The Turn of the Screw* shares with virtually all the classic narratives of the Gothic tradition, from *Otranto* to *Udolpho* to *Jane Eyre* to *The Woman in White*; that is, a narrative void, an empty space, created by the default of the traditional paternal function: not so much the Law of the Father as the Flaw of the Father, due to the absence, death or perverse irresponsibility of the Master of the House. It is the absence or withdrawal of the Master from Bly, his abdication of responsibility, which creates the vacuum or spectral space in which the ghosts appear, just as in his absence he had installed Quint in situ at Bly. (2000: 65)

The first reaction of the governess to Flora was "there could be no uneasiness in a connexion with anything so beatific as the radiant image of my little girl, the vision of whose angelic beauty had probably more than anything else to with the restlessness" (*TotS* 1: 30). Long before her first sighting of any apparitions, she is kept awake and roaming the dark rooms of Bly, responding to "possible" recurring sounds she "fancied" she heard, including "a moment when I believed I recognised, faint and far, the cry of a child." But the children are in danger from their protectors. The governess' language about the children, although matching much Victorian rhetoric about childhood, is always excessive. It is first overly assertive about their physical beauty and perfect behavior, their angelic, extramortal nature. The first-time governess thinks that to "watch, teach, 'form' little Flora would too evidently be the making of a happy and useful life" (31). Flora has "the deep sweet serenity indeed of one of Raphael's holy infants." When Miles returns from school, the governess instantly feels "in the great glow of freshness, the same positive fragrance of purity. . . . He was incredibly beautiful . . . everything but a sort of passion of tenderness for him was swept away by his presence. What I then and there took him to my heart for was something divine . . . his indescribably little air of knowing nothing in the world but love" (3: 36, 37; see also 4: 43). It would be impossible for any children to stay in such heavenly realms over the course of months of daily contact, but there is no middle course of mere normality in the governess' descriptions of them. They are moved from innocence and purity to sinful knowledge, collusion with evil spirits, and amorality. Their surface beauty masks their inner corruption from which the governess alone must save them. But she realizes suddenly she is too late: her lamentations overflow into Mrs. Grose's "motherly breast." She sobs in despair, "I don't save or shield them! It's far worse than I dreamed. They're lost!" (7: 59; see also 13: 81). Ruth Yeazell has argued that all of James's fiction is centered on "journey from innocence to experience, a secular Fall" (Yeazell 1976: 33).

Many of the governess' interactions with always surprised, tentative, and hesitant Mrs. Grose are devoted to coercing the illiterate housekeeper into accepting the governess' visions and collaborating into protecting Miles and Flora from the dead former servants (at least through constant surveillance). Her descriptions of these exchanges are consistently self-congratulatory, always making every sign or declaration with Mrs. Grose a "vow" or pledge of tacit communication and loyalty (see *TotS* 1: 32; 3: 37). According to the narrator, Mrs. Grose "accepted without directly impugning my sanity the truth as I gave it to her. . . . 'He was looking for little Miles.' A portentous clearness now possessed me. '*That's* whom he was looking for.' 'But how do you know?' 'I know, I know, I know.' My exaltation grew. 'And you know, my dear'" (6: 50). But Mrs. Grose is a reluctant witness, unwilling to give any more than hints and tacit allowances, pregnant pauses, to the relentless interrogations of the governess, who leads the witness and fills in the blanks (see 8: 62). She connects Miles with Quint and Flora with Miss Jessel, each innocent paired with one of the "wretches" in the transgressive couple. Forcing yet another "admission" from the housekeeper, the governess feels the new information "suited exactly the particular deadly view I was in the act of forbidding myself to entertain" (63). Sometimes the governess recognizes she is forcing her reading of evil on Mrs. Grose but is always certain that reflects Mrs. Grose's lack of intelligence and imagination rather than the fact that the governess' evidence is only what she herself believes she has seen. "I had made her a receptacle of lurid things, but there was an odd recognition of my superiority—my accomplishments and my function—in her patience under my pain" (11: 73; see also 12: 76–7 and 19: 100: "the chain of my logic was ever too strong for her"). Always she sees herself involved with heroic self-sacrifice: "something within me said that offering myself bravely as the sole subject of such experience, by accepting, by inviting, by surmounting it all, I should serve as an expiatory victim and guard the tranquillity of the rest of the house-hold. The children in especial I should thus fence about and absolutely save" (*TotS* 6: 50–1, see also 22: 111). The governess' sense of her heroism grows with each encounter she has with Quint. She feels victorious, exalted, with her power over Quint growing and with her belief Quint is aware of her force (see, for examples, *TotS* 6: 53; 8: 62; 9: 66–7; 22: 110).

The governess never sees what the readers of her narrative see: her "proofs" persuade no one, nobody else shares her experiences of seeing the apparitions, and she is rejected by Miles, Flora, and even Mrs. Grose. As the months pass after his expulsion from his school, Miles begins to press the governess for an answer to his schooling (he has clearly already outgrown the governess' educational preparation and her peculiar pedagogy). He finally declares he will write to his uncle and persuade him to visit Bly. Her response is a sort of collapse of confidence that results in her decision "without a scene, without a word," throwing over her position in "cynical flight" (15: 87). Coincidentally, she collapses exactly where a month earlier she believes she had seen Miss Jessel; at the moment of her betrayal of her self-imposed heroic mission, she sees her "vile predecessor" seated at her writing desk. Disappointingly, no one seems to take notice of her flight and when she returns she is "freshly upset at having to find them merely dumb and discreet about my desertion" (87–8). This makes her reconstitute her plan to confront the ghosts and to get Miles to confess what was behind his expulsion from school, although perhaps only most tenuously connected to Peter Quint. What made the governess experience such a violent reaction when Miles declared he would be able to contact the uncle and get him to actually visit Bly? Why shouldn't she welcome turning such a weighty responsibility, as she believed, over to his hands? She has repeatedly lied to Mrs. Grose about writing to him, only pretending to do so to keep her from seeking some other way to communicate with him, and she had the children write letters to him in her classroom that she has in her possession when she writes her manuscript.

She is conscious of her lies about communicating with the uncle; it seems like she must be conscious of lying about her interactions with the apparitions. She tells Mrs. Grose that she just had a talk with Miss Jessel.

> "A talk! Do you mean she spoke?"
> "It came to that. I found her, on my return, in the schoolroom."
> "And what did she say?" I can hear the good woman still, and the candour of her stupefaction.
> "That she suffers the torments—!"
> It was this, of a truth, that made her, as she filled out my picture, gape. "Do you mean," she faltered "—of the lost?"
> "Of the lost. Of the damned. And that's why, to share them—" I faltered myself with the horror of it.
> But my companion, with less imagination, kept me up. "To share them—?"
> "She wants Flora." (*TotS* 16: 90)

Of course, the readers of the governess' manuscript know that none of this is true. She did believe she saw for a moment the sad image of her predecessor seeming to confirm through gesture that the desk and classroom belonged to her and that the governess was made to feel she was the intruder. The "meeting" was wordless. But clearly she believes in the existence of the ghosts since she otherwise would not expose herself to the complete destruction of her months of persuasion by asking Mrs. Grose to witness Miss Jessel appearing at the lake. All of her earlier imaginary victories are reversed: "with this hard blow of the proof that her eyes were hopelessly sealed I felt my own situation horribly crumble." Finally Mrs. Grose is unequivocal, rushing away repulsed and disgusted, exclaiming, "I see nobody. I see nothing, I never *have*. I think you're cruel. I don't like you!" (20: 103). Yet there is a partial victory; even though Mrs. Grose didn't see the ghost, with her small imagination and sealed eyes, and even though Flora will never speak to the governess again. Despite this, the "horrors" and never specified "things" Flora confides to Mrs. Grose cause the housekeeper to believe in the evil influences. She agrees to flee with Flora, taking her away from Bly and straight to the uncle while the governess stays to do battle with Quint over Miles. Mysteriously, she still believes she needs only to get Miles to reveal what happened at his school and if he confesses, he will be "saved" (21: 110).

Psychoanalytic approaches to *The Turn of the Screw* represent the major alternative to the traditional ghost story (that accepts the existence of the ghosts and focuses on the horrifying prospect of supernatural corruption of the children). We will discuss the key works that set up the framework for the psychoanalytic discussion more specifically in Chapter 4. During the time of James's experimental and major phases, and then in the decade after James's death, Freud was beginning to publish his case studies of hysteria, infant and child sexual drives, the economy of the unconscious and conscious with its topography of id, ego, libido, and superego, sublimation and displacement, and then the Uncanny. All of these concepts and more provided critics so minded with what seemed keys or tools to the locked box of secrets behind literary texts. In some ways, the supernatural reading of the work was treated through most of the twentieth century as the naïve, surface reading, fine for the unsophisticated. Formalistic approaches, that concentrated on style, structures, genre, and so on (essentially, what we have looked at in Chapter 2), were seen by psychoanalytic readers as ignoring the best, realistic explanation for the bizarre thoughts and fatal actions of the governess. While the nonpsychoanalytic realist might see the governess as mad or delusional and the ghosts as hallucinations, the psychoanalytic critics felt they saw the reasons for her projections as based in her repressed sexuality, her thwarted desire transferred from the master to Quint as the symbol of male sexuality and aggression, to Miles as the embodiment of the master. In addition, psychoanalytic criticism inevitably loops back to the author and so the biographies, notebooks, and letters of James, as they were published through the century, both provided more "evidence" about James's family and sexual conflicts that were now seen as being present throughout his fiction, and the accumulation of these readings seemed to certify the psychoanalytic biographical studies. The success of the proliferating literary readings anchored in Freudian concepts continues to the present time even though contemporary psychiatrists and clinical analysts may have no connection with it. Although practicing clinicians with patients may have little use for Freud and his studies and ideas, they are still actively functional for literary critics, art historians, film scholars, cultural studies, and many others, because the attractions of its explanatory power. With that said, despite the explanatory power and the new techniques of interpretation, the many ambiguities in *The Turn of the Screw* have not been resolved; the tremendous increase of biographical and cultural documents, along with the increased range and interdisciplinarity of studies of the text, have guaranteed a further proliferation of possible paths and answers. Finality is a doubtful, if not suspicious, position.

GENDER, SEXUALITY, AND HYSTERIA

We have focused on the battle between good and evil, the existence of the ghosts (or at least the governess' sincerity in her recount of her meetings with the dead servants), and her self-perception as heroic savior of the children, even though the work ends with Flora being sent to seek safety with the uncle and with Miles dead of apparent heart failure. This reading follows the thinking of the governess as shown in her manuscript. Her version may be sincere even if we decide it is unreliable, that there were no apparitions and in following what she believed was the best course, she caused disaster. This represents the great many readings that are following the traditional genre of the ghost story or else are nonpsychological or historical, "realistic" readings. The psychological interpretations focus on the never-explicit sexual secrets and tensions. Ruth Yeazell argues that "the sexual reticence of his late fiction is in direct proportion to the felt presence of sexuality as a force at the very center of human life. Beginning with the fiction of the late nineties . . . and continuing through *The Sacred Fount* and the novels of the major phase, sexual passion becomes the central mystery, the hidden knowledge which the Jamesian innocent must at last confront" (Yeazell 1976: 20). The 20-year-old first-time governess is herself one of the innocents in this regard. She expunges sexual questions or comments from her conversations with Mrs. Grose, her only confidante, or from her manuscript, and yet it seems everywhere present.

The governess' sexuality is limited, as far as information revealed to the readers, to her imagined relationship with the master of Bly, the uncle of Miles and Flora. In the frame before the governess' narration begins, the frame narrator adds to the reasons Douglas gives for the young woman to take the job "the seduction exercised by the splendid young man. She succumbed to it." When Douglas seems to deny the potential love story by saying she only saw the master twice, the narrator says, "that's just the beauty of her passion." He is surprised Douglas agrees, again speaking directly to the perspicacious narrator (to whom he will later leave the manuscript, a kindred spirit). The reason others turned down the position was because of the main requirement that "she should never trouble him—but never, never: neither appeal no complain nor write about anything . . ., take the whole thing over and let him alone" (*TotS* 28). The governess confided to Douglas that "when, for a moment, disburdened, delighted, he held her hand, thanking her for the sacrifice, she already felt rewarded" (29). This information, which all sounds so discouraging for any possibility of a love story, is essential for her romantic fantasies; she is the agent and stand-in for the absent master; she is constantly rewarded every time she takes on any problems that would cause any less courageous and competent trustee to violate the main condition. She feels he has invested her with his powers at Bly; she has supreme authority. Already, in the moment he shakes her hand, we find the language of sacrifice and reward that appears throughout her narrative. More than the children's governess, she is the queen of the little kingdom of Bly. She notes the children's bloom of "health and happiness" and it is "as if I had been in charge of a pair of little grandees, of princes of the blood . . ., the only form that in my fancy the after-years could take for them was that of a really royal extension of the garden and the park" (3: 38), and it is such fantasies that make tolerable the governess' "small smothered life." Despite the frequent recognition of the excellent qualities of the children (before she realizes they have been trapping her), the governess most enjoys her solitary summer dusk walks.

> I could take a turn into the grounds and enjoy, almost with a sense of property that amused and flattered me . . . doubtless perhaps also to reflect that by my discretion, my quiet good sense and high propriety, I was giving pleasure—if he ever thought of it!—to the person to whose pressure I had yielded. What I was doing was what he had earnestly hoped and directly asked of me, and that I *could*, after all, do it proved even a greater joy than I had expected. I dare say I fancied myself in short a remarkable young woman. (38–9)

Through the increasingly nightmarish circumstances experienced by the governess (whether the ghosts are "real" or are only in her

imagination is irrelevant as far as her emotional trials), from responding to Mile's expulsion to the evil presence of the apparitions, the
governess' response always returns to her fealty to her master and the
pleasure it gives him. The greater the trials, in fact, the greater her
display of loyalty and command, of taking his burdens on herself,
and the greater her pleasure in imagining his, if only he knew. She is
incoherent and adamant in her response to Mrs. Grose's demands to
contact the master and ask him to come to Bly and solve the problems; she declares she would leave the children and the estate immediately. The governess is distraught to think of the master's "derision,
his amusement, his contempt for the breakdown of my resignation at
being left alone and for the fine machinery I had set in motion to attract
his attention to my slighted charms . . . how proud I had been to serve
him and to stick to our terms" (12: 78). The children also begin hinting
their uncle might visit, investing the absent master with almost religious
hopes and mystery. Frequently one or the other of the children will
raise "the precious question that had helped us through many a peril.
'When do you think he *will* come?' . . . 'He' of course was their uncle
in Harley Street; and we lived in much profusion of theory that he
might at any moment arrive to mingle in our circle" (13: 82). The governess knows this will not happen because of the "doctrine" which was
the main condition by which she is allied to him. "He never wrote to
them . . . it was part of the flattery of his trust of myself; for the way in
which a man pays his highest tribute to a woman is apt to be but the
more festal celebration of one of the sacred laws of his comfort." In
only pretending to mail Miles's and Flora's letters to their uncle, the
governess is certain she "carried out the spirit of the pledge not to
appeal to him." The religious terminology and temporal authority meld
with the romantic language: "attract his attention to my slighted
charms," "the way in which a man pays his highest tribute to a woman."

From his earliest appearance in the book, 10-year-old Miles is presented as a protogentleman, substituting for her imaginary liaison
with the uncle. When she is most concerned in acting as a "gaoler,"
keeping the children under constant surveillance to prevent them
from perhaps falling under the influence of the dead servants, he
seems most mature and ready to assert his primacy. She realizes,
"Turned out for Sunday by his uncle's tailor, who had had a free
hand and a notion of pretty waistcoats and of his grand little air,
Miles's whole title to independence, the rights of his sex and situation, were so stamped upon him that if he suddenly struck for freedom

I should have had noting to say" (*TotS* 14: 83). His hints that he wants to return to a school, that he cannot spend all of his time with the governess and little sister, is not only an acknowledgment of the governess' limitations in her own knowledge, but a rejection of the romantic idyll of the young governess and the uncle. Her first response is not to the school issue at all but to feel unattractive ("I seemed to see in the beautiful face with which he watched me how ugly and queer I looked," 84). Miles announces that he is "a fellow" who is getting on and the governess immediately sinks into helplessness. He later asks her about the "queer business" of the way she is attempting to bring him up (17: 92). The romantic rejection by Miles prefigures the rejections by Mrs. Grose and Flora to her strategies as a guard against evil. Although she had been content up until this time to avoid asking him anything about whatever occurred at his school to cause his expulsion, now that suddenly becomes the uppermost secret that needs to be divulged. They had both been, she believes, happy in staying in the present moment, this particular day at Bly, with no discussion of anything that happened prior to his return there (and she is free of her own identity and history prior to becoming the agent of the uncle). His frequently mentioned politeness and decorum now seems suspect to her: "It was extraordinary how my absolute conviction of his secret precocity—or whatever I might call the poison of an influence that I dared but half-phrase—made him . . . appear as accessible as an older person, forced me to treat him as an intelligent equal" (93). The earlier notions of angelic innocence fray and then are completely destroyed in tandem with the end of the romantic fantasy and she becomes harsh and vengeful. The repeated phrase "little gentleman," as applied to Miles and connecting him with the uncle, becomes mixed with a new sense of Miles as Quint's "dark prodigy" and she no longer is concerned that Miles is out of her sight and left alone with Quint in the classroom (18: 96, 97). After Mrs. Grose has fled Bly with Flora, just prior to climactic scene of making "a new plunge into the hideous obscure," the governess is left with Miles. The honeymoon imagery that enters the governess' mind seems more dark than whimsical: "We continued silent while the maid was with us—as silent, it whimsically occurred to me, as some young couple whom on their wedding-journey, at the inn, feel shy in the presence of the waiter" (22: 113).

In Chapter 2 we pointed out the tangled narrative situation of a male character reading a manuscript written by a female character in a text by a male author using a female persona. We can now see that the female narrator assumes the authority of the male, the master, taking on a male mask; she both identifies with him and is bound in her acceptance of his trust. Her gratification comes through imagining the pleasure he would experience if he knew all that she was enduring or the dangers she was combating for his sake. His silence is the demonstration of his absolute trust in her; her silence is her proof that she is able to carry out the extraordinary condition he placed on her. This elaborate structure exists only in the governess' mind; we have no information available about the actual intentions or thoughts of the uncle at all. He never appears in the story after hiring her in Harley Street except as a silence, an absent potential power, a judge. But the elegance of this construction is disrupted by the maturing of Miles during this five-month period and his assertion of being a fellow who needs freedom, who has outgrown the governess' tutoring, who had a "secret precocity." This returns once again to whatever happened at the school, finally coerced out of Miles in the closing pages. He finally admits saying things to those he liked, and that they repeated those things to those they liked. Such a vague, bland confession momentarily rattles the governess:

> Those he liked? I seemed to float not into clearness, but into a darker obscure, and within a minute there had come to me out of my very pity the appalling alarm of his being perhaps innocent. It was for the instant confounding and bottomless, for if he *were* innocent what then on earth was I? . . . "Stuff and nonsense! . . . What *were* those things?" My sternness was all for his judge, his executioner. (24: 119)

She cannot accept the confession she has forced from him because if this is all there is, then she has been wrong and Miles and Flora are innocent. If they are innocent, it must mean that she was wrong about the apparitions and their evil influence. When this momentary doubt enters, she thinks she may well release Miles from surveillance and protection, that he could go to the window because there are no ghosts waiting for him. She must reject that and at once sees at the window, "as if to blight his confession and stay his answer, was the hideous author of all our woe," Quint. Miles clearly sees nothing; attempting to give the governess the answers she requires to release him, he thinks she sees Miss Jessel. Wrong! He tries again and asks, "It's *he*?"

I was so determined to have all my proof that I flashed into ice to challenge him. "Whom do you mean by 'he'?"

"Peter Quint—you devil!" His face gave again, round the room, its convulsed supplication. "*Where*?"

"There are in my ears still, his supreme surrender of the name and his tribute to my devotion." (120)

This phrasing is similar to the way religious and sexual vocabulary is blended in the governess' description of giving pleasure to the absent master by carrying out her pledge. Quint and Miss Jessel must have the existence and terrible impact she has already posited or everything she has thought, and everything that has created the importance of her position and her secret liaison with the master is suddenly, horribly wrong. The death of Miles is preferable to having to admit that she has been wrong in all of her interpretations and thinking. It is ironic that she describes Quint as "the author of all our woe," when the governess is doubly that author.

Perhaps there has been too little attention paid to the governess as the author of the main narrative. Recent gender criticism of James has drawn attention to the issues of authority, suppressed voices, master and mastery, identity, masculinity and femininity (as well as the fragility of such boundaries). The artistry and careful craftsmanship and stylistic control has been attributed to James, not to the putative author. The ambiguities, narrative gaps, and unsaid is blamed on the narrator of the main text, her hysteria, her fear of being wrong, her youth, and provincialism. How has she crafted her narrative and structured it artistically, and to what effect? It is not to her a ghost story or even a report of apparitions; it is a confession, a defense, an expiation, a self-analysis, a secret revelation of a long-hidden trauma. Marianne DeKoven has pointed out the many misogynistic stereotypes applied to the governess by critics through the decades (DeKoven 1991: 48–9). DeKoven also argues that the main narrator is usually referred to only as the governess, reserving the title of narrator for the presumed male narrator of the frame. This "fixes the protagonist in, and defines her by, her subordinate class-gender status, of reader-identified selfhood." By contrast, in Joseph Conrad's *Heart of Darkness*, Marlow is always treated as the narrator, not the male "I" of the frame narration (see also McWhirter 1993: 132–3, 146 n. 28). In *Turn of the Screw* criticism, agency and ownership is given to Douglas and it is assumed that the frame narrator is also male, although the text gives no gender clues. As a gendered turn of the screw, Linda Kauffman makes a hypothetical case for the frame narrator to be considered as female instead of just assumed, without evidence, to be male.

> Suppose . . . that the governess' unrequited love for her employer leads her to write her narrative, which she gives to Douglas before she dies; Douglas' unrequited love for the governess replicates her love for her employer; the second narrator loves Douglas as he loves the governess; she re-enacts the governess' writing by making an exact transcript of her narrative, which Douglas commits to her before his death. This transcript is the source of the narrative. It is a "copy" of desire in triplicate, for the governess' desire is copied from *Jane Eyre*, Douglas' is copied from the governess, and the second narrator has made her own copy. (Kauffman 1986: 230)

In speaking now of such doubling, thwarted desire as the motive for narrative (as wish-fulfillment in the Freudian dreamwork), and gender-switching voices we can see the acknowledged outer author of the text (James) as the double for the unacknowledged and scorned inner author of the main narrative (the governess) in a text that revolves about unspeakable sexual secrets. David Wagenknecht, connecting *The Turn of the Screw* with Freud's study of hysteria known as "Dora" (1905), sees the work as an allegory,

> a kind of coded lamentation about the grievous loss James feared he had incurred by sacrificing his overt (homo)sexuality. . . . The story is doubtless on one level an allegory to the effect that the wages of homophobia are death. The names of Miles and Flora suggest, inter alia, the genders, and Peter Quint's name just as clearly represents a bi-sexual disposition. (1998: 436, 437)

In Wagenknecht's fertile reading, the story has not one hysteric but two: the governess and the author. With this understanding, the late style of indirection, euphemism, obliquity, and ambiguity are not technical matters of style but instead are an unconscious occlusion of what James holds most deeply hidden about himself. The novels, as Freud argued in "Creative Writers and Daydreaming," are the publicly accepted way for the unacceptable desires and unfulfilled wishes to be given form and shared. In Freud's view, the author cannot realize what his unconscious desires are but acknowledges only his conscious displacement and sublimation of the dreamwork into plays, novels, and other art forms. The audience also reads on the conscious level, speaking of genre and form, considering the realism and satisfactory plot or characters, comparing this with other works. But they are actually responding unconsciously to the memory of their own psychological and sexual conflicts and stages of development.

In her influential reading of *The Turn of the Screw*, Shoshana Felman simultaneously reads Freudian method. If the author of the literary work cannot see the unconscious origination in the hidden subtext, they are themselves inside the texts they create, as well as exterior to them. Similarly, the readers are unaware of their inclusion in the text even prior to their reading. The analyst listens to the fragments of the memories and associations, the meandering and partial bits of dreams, that has been censored before the patient speaks. The analyst's job is to create a coherent narrative and see what cannot be consciously faced by the patient and persuade the patient of the interpretation. That is what effects the cure. Critics and analysts measure their success by mastering the text, and creating a new text (the interpretation) that, through their artistry (their powers to persuade, their tact and delicacy, their authority), will be accepted by the patient or by readers. But the will-to-mastery overcomes the doubts about the truthfulness or validity of the interpretation. It also leads to strategies of emotional distancing and indirection on the part of the analyst who otherwise is caught within the new texts (and putting into infinite deferral the hidden basis of their own interpretations, or their interests in creating). This drive to mastery, and the avoidance of self-revelation, leads psychoanalytic critics down narrow paths to find the one solution. Felman wants to use the rhetoric she finds in Freud and French psychoanalyst Jacques Lacan, to retain ambiguity and openness of interpretation and defer meaning. In addition, she sees, with Jacques Derrida, that there is nothing beyond the text; the interpreter is not exterior any more than the reader or author (Felman 1980). She sees *The Turn of the Screw* as analogous to the psychoanalytic reading. Analyzing the multiple narrators and the language of the work's frame, she argues that "the chain of narrative voices which transmits *The Turn of the Screw* is also, at the same time, a chain of *readings* . . . each narrator, to relay the story, must first be a *receiver* of the story, a *reader* who at once records it and *interprets* it, simultaneously trying to make sense of it and *undergoing* it, as a lived experience, an 'impression,' a *reading-effect*" (Felman 124). The story of the unconscious and its chains of interpretations and transmissions resembles James's text. While there is "seduction" and transference among the narrators who want to maintain the textual chain in its undecidable "thickness," each narrator (and each reader and the author) enacts being both analyst and patient in the interpretive chain. She plays on the uses of the word "grasping" in the description of the death of Miles, to show the multiple roles she plays: "the governess's triumph as a reader as a therapist, both as an interpreter and as an exorcist, is rendered highly suspicious by the death of what she has set out at once to *understand* and to *cure*. It therefore behooves the reader of *The Turn of the Screw* to discover the meaning of this murderous effect of meaning; to understand how a child can be killed by the very act of understanding" (Felman 161).

The arrest and sensational trial of Oscar Wilde brought exaggerated public awareness and scrutiny to homosexuality (including the revelation of wealthy men having sex with young males who were lower-class workers, such as telegraph delivery boys, for money). What was either denied or ignored in late Victorian society was suddenly in newspaper headlines and the courtroom. Convicted under the Criminal Law Amendment Act of 1885 of committing acts of gross indecency, Wilde was given a sentence of five years imprisonment at hard labor. Neill Matheson has provided a succinct analysis of shame in *The Turn of the Screw* in light of the sudden spotlight on homosexuality.

> The story's casting of sexuality in the mode of Gothic terror and its thematizing of the fear of going public are responses to the climate of anxiety surrounding nonnormative sexuality in England in the 1890s. . . . James followed the Wilde trials with both dismayed fascination and a sense of their dramatic interest, as his letters of the time reveal. The Gothic plot of *The Turn of the Screw* provided him with an apt language for representing the complex significations and charged affects surrounding same-sex sexuality made especially salient by the Wilde trials. In fact, Douglass's [*sic*] provocative comments invoking "uncanny ugliness and horror and pain" almost might serve as well as an introduction to the Wilde "scandal" and its effects for James and others. (Matheson 1999: 711)

Everything associated with Wilde, such decadent aestheticism, art-for-art's sake, homoeroticism and androgyny, and ambivalent morality were placed into public scrutiny and suspicion that lasted for decades. James disliked Wilde before the arrest but certainly had some of the interests and habits (such as being a lifelong bachelor, well-to-do, devoted to the arts, effeminate, with an enormous number of close friendships with other men, and so on) that now seemed unacceptable. Some recent critics argue that *The Turn of the Screw* is a "manner of interrogating the fate of Aestheticism in the late 1890s" and that the psychological projection of the "child-adult configuration" in which the child's "conspicuous lack of innocence and moral values generates a nightmarish situation for the adult characters, who struggle in vain to control the children" (Mendelssohn 2007: 242–3). Malcolm Pittock considers *The Turn of the Screw* to be the "ultimate decadent text" (Pittock 2005).

CLASS, HISTORY, AND THE MATERIAL WORLD

There are at least two time periods to consider in reading *The Turn of the Screw*. It is set in the late 1840s and it was published in 1898. Whether read as a ghost story or a psychological story, it reflects the anxieties and issues of the extratextual world, especially class. There are very few characters in the story (functionally, just the group gathered to tell and hear ghost stories in the partial frame, the master and his niece and nephew, and servants) and only three settings (the upper-class house of the frame, the master's Harley Street home in London, and the country estate of Bly). But class consciousness is always an unspoken shared element, an encoded cultural subtext that was so much a part of the lives of the work's characters and the initial readers, it does not need to be overt. For readers more than a century later, however, this is not necessarily so apparent (while class divisions and consciousness exists today, of course, the shared cultural codes have shifted dramatically). We might note, additionally, that "readers" can be considered in various ways. There are those to whom the narrative is addressed or the fictional narratees; these are readers constructed within the text. There are the actual readers of the 1898 serial publication in *Collier's Weekly* and subsequent book publication (including the New York Edition of 1908 with the Author's Preface). Then there are the actual readers of the present time (each reader approaching the text with different personal background including age, sex, class, and nationality, reading knowledge, context for coming to the text, and how the text is itself surrounded by editorial notes and prefaces, illustrations, and whatever is happening in the world beyond the text).

Readers now, considering the violence, crime, poverty, economic turmoil, terrorism, and constant international conflict, might view the second half of nineteenth-century Great Britain with a false nostalgia. Social agitation and clashes throughout Europe (especially in 1848, the year Karl Marx and Friedrich Engels published the *Communist Manifesto*) alarmed conservatives and energized the workers of the new industries leading to often violent strikes. The middle class grew in size and political influence and there was increased democratization (though aristocratic control was still maintained in most realms and women could not vote in Britain or the United States until the 1920s). Every middle-class household could have a number of servants because labor was so cheap and working conditions were unregulated (creating a 70-hour work week or limiting children from the most dangerous occupations were progressive, late century reforms). Beginning in the 1880s, there were assassinations and bombings linked to Irish nationalists and various anarchist or other underground groups that brought terrorism to the fore. Labor unions were formed, there were Socialists elected to office, child labor laws and free public education were established. By the 1890s, it seemed to many that the Empire was in decline, that the new powers must supersede the old. Social reformers focused on the terrible poverty and living conditions of the great majority of the population and a sense of physical and moral "degeneration." The rural areas were increasingly depopulated and the urban areas grew into industrial metropolises (including newly made redbrick milltowns). The reality contradicts the often beautiful, peaceful, luxurious, or bucolic images of Victorian England current readers have taken in through twentieth-century fiction and, more emphatically, films and television series (BBC/PBS and Merchant-Ivory and others).

An important element of Victorian fiction and James's "international theme" is the attitude toward class and aristocracy and the differences between British and American understanding of this. The stratification of class in Britain was seen as permanent, natural, and beneficial, especially by the aristocracy and upper-middle class who were quite content with their places (sometimes the destitute and working poor were less enthusiastic about this philosophy). This was a holdover of the Great Chain of Being; for people, this indicated the divine support of the sovereign and then went descended hierarchically through the ranks of the aristocracy and then the social classes and temporal occupations. Other perfect chains could be constructed on this model for nations or races or animals, and so on. The expansion of the middle class and the nouveau riche industrial giants, along with the far larger population of the poor (especially those finding themselves suddenly displaced from the homes and jobs in the countryside that had been hereditary and lifelong), rubbed against the model of fixed classes. A fabulously successful investor or inventor or a manufacturer could never be an aristocrat; an aristocrat who lost his fortune would still be an aristocrat. A common Victorian plot line dealt with the dangers of marrying outside of one's class (a middle-class person marrying one of the poor, a financially stressed aristocrat taking a title-seeking wealthy spouse, and, in James's fiction, it often meant the attractions and the problems with mixed European and American liaisons). By contrast, the class theme rarely exists in American fiction, following the foundational narrative that anyone could rise (or fall) by their own efforts, abilities, and seizing of opportunities. The plot engines in the Victorian period revolve around lost or damaging wills, dowries, heirs, and heiresses, marriages for property instead of love (the wealthier the characters, the lower the value would be placed on love). The middle class was always yearning to know what the aristocrats did and they imitated what they could (piano lessons and French lessons for girls, Latin and rhetoric for boys, and shared taste for opera, censored versions of Shakespeare, and whatever was the current fashions). Fiction and, to some extent, theater, provided innumerable opportunities for the overwhelmingly middle-class readership of books and journals to peek into the intimate lives of the wealthy and the aristocratic.

The group gathered for the traditional telling of ghost stories in the partial frame of *The Turn of the Screw* are probably much higher in social status than the readers of the popular weekly magazine where the work was published. The audience in the frame (as opposed to the actual readers) grew up with servants of all sorts tending to their needs. They all had governesses (and stories about governesses, complaints and scandals, loyal governesses and failures); the author of the main narrative was Douglas's sister's governess (on historical and cultural contexts of Victorian governess see Bell 1993 as well as *TotS* 123–38). When he decides to read the story, he must write to his "man" to send it up by coach from his London apartments to the country house. They have surrounding them an orderly network of housekeepers, groundskeepers, valets, cooks, maids, and others, as needed, depending on the size of their estates and families and whether they are in the country or the city homes. They drop French phrases into their conversation ("*Raison de plus*—at that age!" [all the more reason, 25]), know that "Trinity" refers to a College of Cambridge University, and must identify themselves with the master of Bly rather than the governess. Douglas's praise of her respectability, or that she was "the most agreeable woman I'd ever known in her position; she would have been worthy of any whatever," is heavily qualified (24). It situates her solely within her job (just as we never learn her name even in the frame). Besides Mrs. Grose, the other servants at Bly are also unnamed and not even mentioned in the governess' narrative: "a cook, a housemaid, a dairywoman, an old pony, an old groom and an old gardener, all likewise thoroughly respectable" (28). It is humorous and revealing that Douglas treats the old pony in the same class as the unnamed servants. Embedded in the households of the wealthy, the servants are constantly necessary but invisible, socially remote and untouchable but intimate, not recognized as personalities but functions. The servants have their own strict hierarchy, like the rigid class structure of the greater world (Mrs. Grose is at the head of the establishment "but belowstairs only" [27]). The constant presence of vaguely noticed servants comes to produce its own fears in the rising middle class and upper class involving sexual temptation or violation that violates class lines (far more significant than sending away a pregnant servant), sexual activity among the servants, and, as another important element in fiction, blackmail by disgruntled or fortune-seeking servants. Governesses as a class had poor reputations among the people who employed them and this explains why Douglas repeats how "respectable" the servants are (and see Millicent Bell on the notion in the Victorian period that their social isolation could drive governesses mad [Bell 1993: 116 n. 11]). But critics who want to discount the psychoanalytic criticism of the governess sometimes do so by talking about the warnings published for the employers about the behavior of servants. For example, Helen Killoran argues that the main secret behind *The Turn of the Screw* is the "sexual rivalry and promiscuity of the servants within the Victorian household" and the story's note of "horror and fear" is caused by such "unrestrained sexuality." She argues that Mrs. Grose and the governess are closer in age than normally thought and they are competing for position and dominance; she sees Mrs. Grose as the figure of evil manipulation who encourages the delusions of the governess in order to regain her dominance over the children and of Bly (Killoran 1993).

When the governess goes to Harley Street for her interview and then to the estate in Essex, she witnesses for the first time from within the sort of fabulous luxury she had earlier known only from fiction. Her reason for becoming a governess matches that of the Brontë sisters, all of whom had to work as governesses: she was presentable, poor, but literate, "the youngest of several daughters of a poor country parson" (26). It is her first position, her first time away from home, her first visit to London, the economic center of the British Empire at its height. His house "impressed her as vast as imposing" (Douglas's audience may not have been impressed with their different position on the social scale). In this prologue, Douglas explains what qualities are needed for his audience to have "a proper intelligence" of the manuscript. It is difficult to judge where Douglas has interpreted and added to what he learned in conversations with the author, and how closely his third-person description hews to her own initial reaction.

> [T]his prospective patron proved a gentleman, a bachelor in the prime of life, such a figure as had never risen, save in a dream or old novel, before a fluttered anxious girl out of a Hampshire vicarage. One could easily fix his type; it never happily, dies out. He was handsome and bold and pleasant, offhand and gay and kind. He struck her, inevitably, as gallant and splendid, but what took her most of all and gave her the courage she afterwards showed was that he put the whole thing as a favour, an obligation he should gratefully incur. She figured him as rich, but as fearfully extravagant—saw him all in a glow of high fashion, of good looks, of expensive habits, of charming ways with women. He had for his town residence a big house filled with the spoils of travel and the trophies of the chase. (26–7)

The ease with which Douglas and his immediate audience (and then the frame narrator and his audience) can place the master as a "type" (and that they are happy this type never dies out) associates them with the master and accepting of his eccentric dealings with the children who have been accidentally thrust upon him, "a lone man without the right sort of experience or a grain of patience." This first encounter is filled with words related to romance rather than to her hiring. Indeed, the entire cash nexus is removed from this meeting. All that she is willing to undergo at Bly is because she is not a mere temporary employee but, as she has apparently convinced Douglas many years after the event, "that he put the whole thing as a favour, an obligation he should gratefully incur." Such an understanding allows the governess to think of herself as a friend and social equal with the master, and to think they have a special and secret relationship that transcends her working for payment. The sexual markers of handsomeness and charming ways with women, of being a wealthy and fashionable bachelor in the prime of life is balanced with markers of power and class, not only his gender but being bold and gallant, "fearfully extravagant," and part of the imperial enterprise. His parents died in India and his younger military brother, father of Miles and Flora, also died, presumably serving or fighting in the colonies. His house being "filled with the spoils of travel and the trophies of the chase" connects him to the Empire, the leisurely life of the aristocracy, the ruthlessness of the hunt; of course, it can also be seen to reflect his presumed sexual conquests.

When the governess arrives at Bly, she is again confused in her reading of class signs and possibilities. Mrs. Grose meets her at the front door and is judged as "a civil person who dropped me as decent a curtsey as if I had been the mistress or a distinguished visitor." The credit redounds not to the housekeeper but to the master: "made me think the proprietor still more of a gentleman, suggested that what I was to enjoy might be a matter beyond his promise" (1: 30). Coming from her poor and crowded home, she is "astonished" by the "liberality with which I was treated." She catalogues all of these new experiences: "The large impressive room, one of the best in the house, the great state bed, . . . the figured full draperies, the long glasses [full-length mirrors] in which, for the first time, I could see myself from head to foot." This first sight of herself is the occasion for assuming her new identity "as if" she was the mistress of Bly (with the double-understanding of mistress as both a sexual companion to a wealthy man and as the legitimate wife). She has such a grand room because Bly is not occupied by its owner and he is not married. But what could be meant by "the great state bed, as I almost felt it" other than that is the place for the principal personage, the master when he visits (at first she has expectations he will visit unannounced, walking up to her when she is walking at dusk). John Carlos Rowe, considering secrecy as a trap for readers that is both a literary technique and an indicator of power structures, finds that this particularly at work in the power discrepancy (and the governess' misreading of her relationship) with the absent master.

> Although his money, property, and position would seem to entitle him to a certain mastery in this culture, the Uncle's refusal to assume any direct responsibility for the care and education of the children makes it easy for critics to trivialize his power as that of some *deus absconditus* who leaves the field open to the Governess. His power in the subsequent narrative is almost exclusively a function of his taboo against communication from the Governess. "He" figures in the text only to the extent that the Governess fears breaking silence. . . . By virtue of his irresponsibility, the Uncle confirms all the more his secret power—itself a power of secrecy and censorship—over the actors at Bly and their audience. (Rowe 1984: 128)

Actually, she is so distant in class from the master that readers would see her romantic thoughts as delusional from the outset, far less likely than having an estate haunted by unhappy spirits. Such liaisons ended in happy marriages in occasional works of fiction (the ur-text for this is Samuel Richardson's *Pamela* or Charlotte Brontë's *Jane Eyre*, published in 1848, at the time the story at Bly is set). In reality, if such an amazing marriage took place, the people and families would be made social outcasts over the broken class boundaries. Once she arrives at Bly, the governess provides almost no information about her parents or siblings or their poverty and problems. We hear once that she has received upsetting news but we never learn what is in the letters she has been getting from her home that is so disturbing. At the same time, her home and family requires no apparent actions from her; the governess is able to forget those troubles because the joy she has from being with the children and taking care of them made it seem that the world did not matter (*TotS* 4: 43–4). The odd isolation of Bly, with no mention of the outside world, not even of any village or neighbors, there are no visitors, and she does not succeed in making the occasional walk to church because of other events. There are no newspapers or journals in the reading matter at Bly; the governess is content with novels from the previous century. A handful of letters arrive at the estate but the governess successfully prevents outgoing letters from leaving the grounds. Jane Eyre is constantly being reminded by others of her social inferiority, her status as a dependent orphan and then a servant, and she notes every slight and cruelty. The artificial isolation of Bly is required for the governess to think of herself as actually the supreme authority in special partnership with the master. This remains her thinking until the closing crises when Miles begins to assert himself and she realizes that he would immediately be recognized, as the male heir, as the de facto master of Bly (14: 83, 85). An important part of the governess' horror in putting together the hints about the sexual relationship between her predecessor and the disreputable former valet is that Miss Jessel was a lady and "he so dreadfully below" (*TotS* 7: 58). Mrs. Grose was alarmed by the impropriety of Miles constantly in company of Quint (not as we might now think because of any fear of sexual transgressions, but because of the vast class difference). She spoke to Miss Jessel about it and was rebuffed. Mrs. Grose felt she had to speak with Miles directly about it saying that "*she* liked to see young gentlemen not forget their station." The governess asks her to confirm, "You reminded him that Quint was only a base menial?" (8: 61, 62). The outward signifier that Quint is not a gentleman is that he does not wear a hat (5: 48). Later, the sign that her predecessor has fallen into disgrace through her liaison with Quint is that Miss Jessel never wears a hat (and the proof that Flora has been the victim of her evil influences is that she also is outside without a hat [18: 97]). The evil influence seems primarily this deliberate ignoring of class boundaries. When the governess tells Mrs. Grose about the man she has seen on the tower, Mrs. Grose asks, almost immediately, "Was he a gentleman?" and the governess instinctively denies it. "'But if he is n't a gentleman—' 'What *is* he? He's a horror'" (5: 46, 47).

The governess' horror with class transgression is almost equal to her disgust with the sexual immorality and corrupting influences of the former servants. Although the term "gentleman" broadened with the expansion of the middle class (who admired men who behaved in "a gentlemanly way"), in the 1840s, when the story is set, a gentleman was one who did not work but who lived from the rents paid to him by the tenants of his lands. If not wearing a hat outdoors is enough of a clue to indicate the class status of the man distantly seen on the tower, someone who accepted a fee for services or who earned money through factories or investments, or if someone worked with his hands, then he was not a gentleman. In the mid-century, surgeons, lawyers, novelists, publishers, owners of mines or mills, were not gentlemen. By the end of the century, the category had become blurred (at least for the middle class and nouveau riche; it remained clear for the old aristocracy). The social rigidity and surprising snobbery of the governess, who had been introduced to us as one of many children of a poor rural parson, as someone who would call the former valet a "base menial," passes by the current reader perhaps without a demurral, even though the former valet was sent by the master as his agent and given no set work, since the master was in London, was able to spend all of his time with the children, rather like the governess. But as we can see from many Victorian sources (both novels by former governesses, such as those of the Brontës, and the documents on the issue gathered in *TotS*), governesses were themselves servants, not considered on a level of social equality to allow them to eat dinner with the family. They were regarded with deep suspicion and there were concerns about the harm they could to their charges (including the sexual temptation they were felt to offer to all of the males of the household). How have we overlooked this? The complete physical and social isolation of Bly is paralleled by the first-person narration; we see through the governess' eyes only and are given the romantic fantasy of a successful crossing of all class barriers.

The governess is acting not only as a substitute for the absent and remote master who cannot be contacted but whose projection of order must be kept by his agent bound by her pledge of loyalty. She is also a replacement for a failed part in the machine, the former governess, Miss Jessel. But Miss Jessel asserts her primacy through being the true possessor of the schoolroom. Her presence in the classroom when the governess has her silent confrontation is more of a defeat for the present governess because she feels the writing desk and the other objects she thought she had inherited are actually still her predecessor's. She realizes as well that there are any number of replacement governesses who will be interviewed in Harley Street and be charmed by the bachelor uncle and take over her exact position. She is also a replacement for Miles' and Flora's mother, never mentioned in the text. John Carlos Rowe, analyzing Douglas's few statements in the prologue about how this bachelor found himself with his dead brother's children, tries out the notion of the illegitimacy of Miles and Flora, showing how the reader can be "duped" by the verbal clues and cultural codes of James's text.

> Seducing the Governess by prohibiting her any further intercourse with him, assigning her *duty* as "supreme authority," communicating with her only be means of unread letters, the Uncle preserves his paradoxical identity: the authority of castration, the power of impotence, the presence of absence. . . . The relation between the Uncle's extravagant authority and the characters' and critics' respectable labors is thus one of exclusion and negation, whereby the dialectic of master and servant is effectively barred and the threat of usurpation forestalled indefinitely. (Rowe 1984: 140)

QUESTIONS

1. We have no explicit statement from the main narrator explaining the motive for telling her story, especially for committing her experiences to paper long after the event. How do you construct her motives for narrating? What are the motives of the other two narrators for transcribing, transmitting, and preserving her story?
2. Do you see *The Turn of the Screw* primarily concerned with the children or with the governess (or perhaps about the dead servants)? Or do you read the text as actually about late Victorian anxieties generally or about James's own repressed sexuality in particular?
3. Pick out some of the particularly vague narrative blanks in the story. What are the ways you might fill in these gaps?

CHAPTER 4

CRITICAL RECEPTION AND PUBLISHING HISTORY

COMPOSITION AND PUBLICATION

It is generally agreed in the biographies that when James felt humili-
ated in the poor crowd reaction at the opening night of his play, *Guy
Domville*, January 5, 1895, he turned away from the theater and
returned to concentrating on fiction. His notebook entry for January
12, 1895, records an anecdote (told "very badly and imperfectly" by
a "lady who had no art of relation, and no clearness") while he was a
guest in the home of the Archbishop of Canterbury two days earlier
(*Complete Notebooks* 1987: 109; reprinted in *TotS* 15 and *NCE* 112).
The anecdote lacked many details but the central idea is clearly the
basis of *The Turn of the Screw*. In the notebook entry, it is clear that
the wicked servants "corrupt and deprave the children; the children
are bad, full of evil, to a sinister degree." The servants die and return
as apparitions to haunt the house and try to tempt the children into
dangerous situations so they might destroy themselves. There is no
ambiguity on the "reality" of the ghosts in this original germ of the
idea. The surprising omission is there is governess who is not mentioned. Instead, in this first note, James thinks that the story should
be told "by an outside spectator, observer." James did not write the
story for more than two years, dictating it during the fall of 1897 to
his stenographer William MacAlpine, completing it in December. He
interrupted work on *What Maisie Knew* to work on *The Turn of the
Screw*, and soon after completing this work, he wrote "In the Cage."

The Turn of the Screw was published serially *Collier's Weekly* in
12 installments from January through April, 1898. It was then published

in book form along with the short story "Covering End" in a volume called *Two Magics* (London: Heinemann, 1898). It was reprinted in 1908 in volume 12 of the New York Edition (along with "The Aspern Papers," "The Liar," and "Two Faces"). James expands upon the notebook entry in his preface to this volume (excerpted in *TotS* 179–86 and *NCE* 123–9). The many editions since that time have reprinted the text from the New York Edition. There are very few revisions between the serial publication and the New York Edition except for punctuation and single words (which is not the case with earlier texts such as *Daisy Miller*; "significant" or "major" variant readings are conveniently provided in charts in *NCE* 89–93 and *OWC* 265–6). It still amounts to about 200 alterations. But the revisions have been the subject of heated debate for many years. Although there is agreement about the facts (what changes were made in the New York Edition), there is disagreement of the interpretation that can be given to them: what is the gist or the cumulative effect of these changes for the readers of the text? Not surprisingly, the editors find that the revisions support their particular camp in the division of those who think the ghosts are "real" and those who think the ghosts are hallucinations or projections of the governess. For example, Leon Edel, the major editor and biographer of James for more than forty years, supported the psychoanalytic readings and argues that the revisions make subtle indications of the unreliability and mental instability of the governess and that the ghosts are her hallucinations. This was widely repeated in criticism as a certainty until E. A. Sheppard, in 1974, denounced this as a "chain of errors" (Sheppard 1974: 252–61). Sheppard argues that the ghosts as "real" and the governess as reliable. For Sheppard, the changes are merely stylistic and reinforce the nonpsychological reading.

The Turn of the Screw has been James's most popular work ever since its initial publication. It has been continually in print in both British and American editions, and has been translated and published around the world. No doubt the combination of its brevity and genre (as ghost story or horror story or as canonical modernist text) has contributed to the flow of editions. It has been published both on its own in small books such as the current Dover Thrift Edition and it has been published, in its entirety, in innumerable anthologies. One reason works of criticism give references to the New York Edition is because of its stability; it has remained static while all other editions have gone in and out of print, were perhaps carelessly edited and proofread, or, if they were primarily meant to be used by students in college courses, they were revised every few years and the pagination would be different with each new edition. But few students are likely to find and use the volumes of the New York Edition from 1908 (nor is it usually necessary since that is the source text for the reliable republications). The current texts most widely used include the ones I have referred to in the first two paragraphs of this chapter and elsewhere in this book. They need not be ranked since they are quite different from one another in both form and contents and serve different purposes.

The Bedford/St. Martin's edition, edited by Peter G. Beidler, includes a historical and biographical introduction and sixty pages of cultural documents (primary material from the Victorian period on children and servants, governesses, apparitions and cases of "demonic possession," illustrations from by John Le Farge from the first publication of the story in *Collier's Weekly*, five reviews of the first book publication, letters from James to acquaintances responding to the book, and an excerpt from the preface to the work in the New York Edition). It also includes a brief critical history, introductions to five different critical approaches, and then applications of these approaches to the work. Finally, there is a brief critical glossary. In the second edition, published in 2004, the approaches are reader-response criticism, psychoanalytic criticism, gender criticism, Marxist criticism, and a combination of approaches, each by a different scholar. The Norton Critical Edition, edited by Deborah Esch and Jonathan Warren, in the second edition, published in 1999, includes a textual history and notes, a brief section of documents by James on the supernatural and ghost stories, a section of James's notebook entries and correspondence about *The Turn of the Screw*, illustrations by Charles Demuth from 1917 and 1918 (after James's death), and about one hundred and twenty pages of critical writing on the book from 1898 to the mid-1990s. The Oxford World Classics edition, reprinted in 2008, is edited by T. J. Lustig, author of *Henry James and the Ghostly* (1994). This places *The Turn of the Screw* in a different sort of context by publishing along with it three other ghost stories by James ("Sir Edmund Orme," "Owen Wingrave," and "The Friends of the Friends"). It includes a critical introduction and relevant excerpts from the prefaces and James's notebooks.

CONTEMPORARY REVIEWS AND EARLY CRITICISM (1898–1930)

Upon its book publication in 1898 (in the volume *Two Magics*), and then freshly in 1908 with the republication in the New York Edition, *The Turn of the Screw* was reviewed by many scores of American and British newspapers and journals. Robin Hoople's book-length study of the critical reception of *Distinguished Discord: Discontinuity and Pattern in the Critical Tradition of* The Turn of Screw (1997) does valuable work in gathering providing context and in locating these now-obscure and rare early reviews, but it is rather digressive and eccentrically organized. These first reviews appear in a section called "naïve public reading" but this belied by the text. A naïve reader has a small background in reading and comes to a text without preconceptions of the work. The audience of *Collier's Weekly* or those who purchased James's book would be the naïve audience; professional book reviewers publishing in the newspapers and magazines cannot be called naïve. The truly naïve readers tend not to write and so we do not have their initial reactions preserved for later study. In fact, an important point made again and again in this section is that these first reviewers were thoroughly familiar with the genre of both the Gothic and the ghost story and aware of the conventions and of other contemporary writers of ghost stories, such as M. R. James; reviewers were reminded of Robert Louis Stevenson's *Dr. Jekyll and Mr. Hyde* (1886) and Bram Stoker's *Dracula* (1896). They knew about psychical research and how cases of apparitions were reported. They were largely familiar with many other works by James and could comment about the development of his later ornate and oblique style compared to his more open earlier stories. They were also reading James's new novel along with whatever novels by other writers were being coming to their attention in 1898 or 1908. James did have a long-established career by this time and had both admirers and detractors, some who thought he was a distinguished and original writer and some who found his work incomprehensible or only sporadically worthwhile. Unlike readers coming to the text today, however, they didn't know James's work after *The Turn of the Screw*. They didn't know how James's status would grow through the rest of century. They didn't know Freud and psychoanalytic theory or all of the other theories and approaches critics would employ during the next century, they were not trained in doctoral programs, but they were not naïve.

The early reviewers focused on the ghosts and the evil possession of the children (see the excellent selection of excerpts from the reviews in *NCE* 149–60). The majority responded to the threatened corruption and the hints of the dead servants' example and illicit sex (even more unmentionable in the newspapers and journals than in James's novel) with declarations of the work's success at eliciting a thrill of horror. James was praised with knowing how to convey the terrifying notion of the destruction of the innocent children who were prematurely brought into sexual knowledge, at the very least through the perverse examples and perhaps verbal tutelage of the Miss Jessel and Quint both before and after their deaths. Like the children, the governess is seen as a perfect innocent struggling with loyalty and devotion against a horrifying and incessant campaign to make them fall; her narration is taken as entirely reliable and James shows particular art in revealing her plight so believably. Some found it was a masterfully crafted work even if they disliked the story itself. The vagueness of the nature of the servants' evil and how precisely they influenced the children is entirely acceptable to the reviewers; the hints are already too terrible. The reviewer in the *New York Times* is representative of this view: "But to the contention that this seemingly frail story—with a theme which would surely fail of effect and might become simply ludicrous in the hands of almost anyone of its author's contemporaries—is one of the most moving and in its implied moral, most remarkable works of fiction published in many years, we steadfastly cling" (quoted in Hoople 1997: 39).

But there was an equally strong reaction against such a repulsive and disgusting story; many professed that the unanswered mysteries and the convoluted style left them not sure about what happened or if they could follow, or wanted to follow, these terrible pathways. For those who were repulsed by the sexual contamination and apparent amorality, this was itself a dangerous work that should be kept out of the hands of moral readers. Just as the governess chided herself for making Mrs. Grose the receptacle of her lurid discoveries, the innocent readers are tainted by being exposed to the perversity in James's tale. As with Thomas Hardy's novels of the 1890s (especially *Tess of the D'Urbervilles* and *Jude the Obscure*), which were naturalistic works without the supernatural scaffolding of James's story, the lack of a clear and directing moral message, as well as the lack of poetic justice (in which the good and evil are rewarded or punished in proportion to their choices and acts), meant the work itself was vicious. At almost the same time James published *The Turn of the Screw*, Hardy stopped writing fiction altogether after the repeated outcry against his work (although he lived until 1930). The indirect clues and numerous gaps and ambiguities that were resolved in positive terms by those who praised the work as masterwork exhibiting great emotion and compassion were filled in completely opposite direction by those who condemned the work. They were suspicious of the improprieties hidden by James's difficult and oblique style. Such reviewers saw what was insinuated behind these empty spots in the text as perverse and unnatural. The Boston Public Library banned the book in 1901, as they had so many others, and were mocked for this by the *Washington Post* (reported in Hoople 1997: 64–5).

The publication of *The Turn of the Screw* in 1908 and then James's death in 1916 were two occasions for longer critical articles and even the first short books devoted to James. One, by the novelist Ford Madox Hueffer (later changed to Ford Madox Ford) in 1913, was the first, apparently, to fault the master of Bly for his irresponsibility which "exposes 'the English habit of leaving young children to the care of improper maids and salacious ostlers'" (Hoople 1997: 99). This was a period of reassessing James's overall achievements and flaws, reviewing his enormous oeuvre and using James's critical writing to understand his aesthetic stance. The Preface written for the New York Edition became attached to that text and was reread for authorial intention and backing of different, greatly varied, critical assessments. But authors cannot control their reputations, especially postmortem (short of returning as ghosts). James's critical fortune matched the history of literary criticism. Although James could never have predicted the twists and turns critical theory and schools of criticism would take, his work has been successively taken up as exemplary for each approach. In this he matches a small group of "high modernist" authors and texts: Joseph Conrad's *Heart of Darkness* (1898), James Joyce's *Ulysses* (1922), T. S. Eliot's *The Waste Land* (1922) (interestingly, like James, these were all expatriated or exiled authors). These authors, along with the proponents of the new modernist aesthetics such as Virginia Woolf and Ezra Pound, saw James as their immediate predecessor and model who was breaking the mold of the Victorian novel, subtly undermining the popular genres like the Gothic or the ghost story, and providing complex and multivalent texts that needed to be reread in a variety of ways; they saw his experiments (as Conrad's, or to go some other nineteenth-century antecedents, Walt Whitman, Gustave Flaubert, Emily Dickinson, Gerard Manley Hopkins, and Herman Melville, brought out triumphantly in the 1920s and 1930s after having been banned, unpublished, ahead of their audiences).

It is not surprising to find at this time the first arguments about the reality of the ghosts and the alternative reading of the ghosts as manifestations of symptoms from the mind of the governess, and that the new field of psychoanalysis provided ways to discuss this. Freud's *The Interpretation of Dreams* and his many other books, including his own popular lectures, were the subject of articles in the newspapers and journals; the modernist authors all leaped to study what seemed to reveal the workings of the unconscious, the neuroses and drives, and the way elements prior to conscious memory or even self-awareness were determinative of behavior throughout a person's life. D. H. Lawrence published an entire book introducing Freud's work to English-language readers. Virginia Woolf's experimental small press, Hogarth, published the collected edition of Freud in English (oddly, though, despite her many breakdowns and suicide attempts, she did not go to a psychoanalyst but followed a regime of isolation and removal of excitement that dated back to the mid-nineteenth century). This was a time in the novel when authors were moving further inward than even James's "centers of consciousness" and attempting to represent the unconscious which was seen as the vaster and deeper mystery. In 1918, Ezra Pound edited a special issue of an important magazine of the modernist avant-garde, the *Little Review*, is credited with being the first commentator to connect Freud with *The Turn of the Screw*. Pound is negative about the way this text, "a Freudian affair which seems to me to have attracted undue interest . . . because of its subject matter . . . the obscenity of 'The Turn of the Screw' has given it undue prominence." He warns that "one must keep to the question of literature and not to irrelevancies" (quoted in Hoople 1997: 101; see also Sheppard 1974: 21). That Pound felt such readings had become a distraction to seeing the texts indicates how deeply psychoanalytic concepts had already entered public discourse and perceptions even prior to publication of scholarly essays in journals by academic critics. So other claimants to the earliest readings of the *Turn of the Screw* as revealing the governess' thwarted sexual desire as the cause of her hallucinations, such as Harold Goddard's 1920 article that remained unpublished until 1957 (long after this was the orthodox view of the story) or the 1923 article by F. L. Pattee on the victimization of the children by the insane governess, as well as Edna Kenton's 1924 essay arguing that the ghosts represent the inner struggles of the governess, are equally steps toward the "all-stops-removed" approach of Edmund Wilson in 1934 (the Goddard and Kenton essays are excerpted in *NCE* 161–70). In her 1921 article, Virginia Woolf concentrates on the silence and unspeakable and the way horror grows in *The Turn of the Screw*. She asks, "Can it be that we are afraid? But it is not a man with red hair and a white face whom we fear. We are afraid of something unnamed, of something, perhaps, in ourselves" (*NCE* 160). We can admire the masterly storytelling when we reexamine it in safety, note "how beauty and obscenity twined together worm their way to the depths—still we must own that something remains unaccounted for." The exact order does not seem to matter since these don't seem influenced by each other as much as they demonstrate the way Freud's work came to fill the discursive space of the 1920s and 1930s.

MID-CENTURY AND BEYOND (1930–1975)

The dominant form of literary criticism that developed in the late 1920s and 1930s was a sort of Formalism that came to be known as New Criticism. It was heavily influenced especially by T. S. Eliot's essays on dissociation of the literary work from the author or from the emotional effect on the audience ("Hamlet and His Problems" and "Tradition and the Individual Talent"), as well as his attacks on Victorian and Romantic literature generally, and his close analysis of difficult poets who had been ignored in the nineteenth century, such as seventeenth-century court poets such as John Donne. The aesthetic value of the New Critics focused on the notion of organicism (that form and content are entirely integrated, that there be no elements in excess, and that nothing was lacking to all the work to achieve a single unified effect). This resulted in an entire recasting of the canon of literature, reordering the previously held hierarchy of literary works. The narrative and declamatory poets beloved in the Victorian period (such as Alfred, Lord Tennyson) or the digressive and bulky novels that had numerous subplots and omniscient narrator commentary and guidance (Dickens, Thackeray, Trollope) were overturned (or relegated to being for the mass audience, while the sophisticated reader would seek out works that fit the new criteria). The most prized works were those that demonstrated complexity, irony, compactness, parts were used to discover the whole and the whole was used to understand the parts. Extratextual reference was never required in great work (though the reader was expected to know all of the meanings of all of the words and languages, as well as have an internal command of the monuments of all of the world's literatures from all time). Under such academic critics as Robert Penn Warren, Cleanth Brooks, and I. A. Richards, this became the dominant mode of criticism in the United States from the 1930s until about 1970 (it entered other countries at various times, coming into France in the beginning of the 1960s where structuralism and semiotics created a welcoming ground). We can see that the values of New Criticism perfectly suited *The Turn of the Screw*; Ian Watt even performed an admired New Critical reading of the first paragraph of James's novel *The Ambassadors*, showing that every theme and important motif of the novel was forecast by the that paragraph and that nothing in that large work is out of place or superfluous. How much easier this was to do with a work as comparatively brief and focused as *The Turn of the Screw*! Similarly, this was the argument for the other modernist authors, and the more complex and experimental the better. The New Criticism was institutionalized through a series of textbooks. The goal became producing new readings of any particular text in order to show what is really the one, unified effect. If this could not be done, then either the work was flawed or the interpreter was incapable. Every element of form, style, and technique was open to being the pivot of a new critical argument.

The other dominant approach applied to *The Turn of the Screw* was psychoanalytic criticism. This opposes formalist aesthetics in most ways. It may not deal with all or even most of a work, but just concentrate on a particular unresolved question, an interpretive knot (why does Hamlet delay in killing Claudius? Why does the governess believe she sees ghosts?). Instead of the work being autonomous, cut off from both life of the author and the emotional response of the reader, for a psychoanalytic critic, all of the ancillary texts of the author (diaries, correspondence, notebooks, drafts of manuscripts [lacking in this case since all of James's works after 1897 were dictated and typed]) can be used to help see the glimpses of the unconscious. Similarly, all of the other works created by the author can be brought in to help direct the reading or provide "evidence." As the product of the author is studied, the works are used to study the author (why did James use the style of indirection and value blanks and gaps? What drew him to this situation and characters?).

The landmark Freudian reading of *The Turn of the Screw* was published by Edmund Wilson in 1934 (several times revised and expanded by Wilson until 1959). Her hysteria is conveyed to the children and the ghosts are simply her hallucinations caused by her sexual repression and confused, impossible infatuation with the master displaced into the figure of the dead valet. Bly is filled with so many phallic or female symbols, the repressed sexual subtext becomes clear: "Observe . . . the significance of the governess' interest in the little girl's pieces of wood and of the fact that the male apparition first takes shape on a tower and the female apparition on a lake." As a ghost story it is insignificant, Wilson asserts, but as a study of "morbid psychology" it is a masterpiece. It fits in with James's oeuvre as a variation on what Wilson describes as the theme of the "frustrated Anglo-Saxon spinster; and we remember that he presents other cases of women who deceive themselves and others about the sources and character of their emotions." It reflects James's own sexual repression and self-censorship. Numerous amplifications and refinements of this essay were published by others, focusing on the insanity or hysteria of the governess and the victimization of the children, including killing Miles with fright. As massive, multivolume scholarly biographies were published by Leon Edel and later Fred Kaplan, and these were themselves imbued with the psychoanalytic method, and as more of James's correspondence and family materials were unearthed, the approach seemed difficult to shake and was always opposed to the formalist analyses. Wilson believed he was solving the ambiguities of the text and in doing so providing a master key to the author and all of his other difficult works. In Chapter 3, the two camps fell out along those who accepted the reality of the ghosts and those who saw the ghosts only as hallucinations or projections of the governess. The many dozens of psychoanalytic readings of *The Turn of the Screw*, most of them more sophisticated and well-read in Freud than was Wilson, generated an equal number of refutations (this has been particularly well covered in Hoople 1997: 150–208).

RECENT TRENDS

The impasse was broken in the mid-1970s by the expansion of critical approaches, many of them directly opposing the goals and aesthetics of New Criticism, rebelling against the decades of dominance. This was certainly related to the political and social movements beyond the university, especially after 1968. Traditional Freudian psychoanalytic criticism also came under attack at this time for its patriarchal and male prejudices, its overly narrow focus (and the scientific rejection of Freud's approach that upheld this). Suddenly the literary canon was being revised constantly and locally. The critical approaches, some of which passed only fleetingly through literature departments before being displaced by or combined with other methods, included reader response, feminist criticism, new historicism, semiotics, structuralism, narratology, deconstruction, Foucaultian archaeologies of discourse and power, Lacanian psychoanalysis, gender studies, queer studies, cultural studies, phenomenological criticism, Marxist criticism, and postcolonialism. All of these have in different ways combined with one another or fought to correct what the other methods seemed to omit or belittle. At the same time, the traditional approaches (including formalism, biography, and literary history) have articulated with the newer approaches. All of these have been applied to James's work.

The single most important essay on *The Turn of the Screw* is, by consensus of the various Jamesian critical histories, Shoshana Felman's 1977 article "Turning the Screw of Interpretation." More than one hundred pages long, this combined Jacques Lacan's psychoanalysis and Jacques Derrida's deconstruction to attack the reductionism and bias of Edmund Wilson's reading, the relationship between psychoanalysis and literature (so that literature is used to question and interpret psychoanalysis instead of the other way around), and the goal of solving the puzzle of James's text. In keeping with many of these approaches, there is an acceptance, even an embrace, of Derrida's ideas of an infinite number of signifiers that have no signifieds, that there may be a permanent doubt (aporia), or that there needn't be a choice between the binary A or B but instead the "answer" is both A and B. The new works on ambiguity in James do not resolve the ambiguities but celebrate and expand them (see Brooke-Rose 1976–1977; Rimmon 1977; Rowe 1984). What had been for decades the complacently accepted is placed under doubt, surrounded by quotation marks of suspicion. Alliances are made among critical approaches not to give the definitive and unequivocal reading, but to expand the potential meanings and significations of the text. So-called nonfiction and other documents, previously viewed as objective and evidentiary are now viewed as having agendas, supporting certain narratives and systems of power. Felman's article stands for this change in *The Turn of the Screw* studies in the same way Wilson's article presented a challenge, using a completely new vocabulary and perspective, to the traditional reading of the ghost story. The same expansion of criticism took place at the same time with all of the other modernist authors and others who had previously been ignored under New Criticism.

As indicated by the reading in Chapter 3, the main areas of recent work on James in general and *The Turn of the Screw* as a recurrent example text, has been in gender and queer studies on the one hand and focus on class, history, and the material world on the other. Henry James had long been a figure of ambivalent sexuality, intense privacy, and associated with fin-de-siècle homosexuality and homoeroticism. The thousands of pieces of correspondence suppressed by both the James family for as long as possible and by Leon Edel's careful selection of the letters for his edition fed the interests of gender and queer studies scholars as they interpreted each newly revealed note. James's own act of burning his letters and asking his correspondents to destroy any of his letters they had in their possession certainly encouraged speculation. The jury is still out on whether or not James ever was sexually active with anyone but that has not slowed the critical pursuit of the range of questions involving sexuality in his works and life (see DeKoven 1991; Freedman 1990; Haralson 2000; Kauffman 1986; Mendelssohn 2007; Ohi 2007; Savoy 2007; Stevens 1998; Walton 2004).

During New Criticism, questions about class, power, and the world reflected in the literary works were all considered to change the focus of the literary critic to some other, unrelated discipline. While doctrinaire Marxist criticism is far rarer now than it was in 1968, James's work has been of great interest to those who are studying power, societal structure, family relationships, nationalism, race, and the political. His transatlantic status and cosmopolitanism, awareness of social and national identity, and, as a permanent expatriate, his outsider status, all have been growing areas for critical interest. He had his own prejudices and snobbishness, as we would expect for anyone of his class and time, but he was always observing society and revealing through his incessant writing what he perceived in the world (see Buelens and Aijmer 2007; McMaster 1988; Robbins 1984; Rowe 2007; Wilson 2005).

QUESTIONS

1. How does the history of critical controversy and changes over a century impact your own reading of the text? When it comes to you with such a body of interpretations, in texts surrounded by prefaces, essays, and scholarly notes, is it possible to experience the text in a fresh way?

2. Study one critical approach you never have considered using and then reread *The Turn of the Screw* as if you are fully committed to the approach you have chosen. What did you see you hadn't noticed before this experiment?

3. What does the history of readings of *The Turn of the Screw* indicate about readers of 1898, the 1950s, and the twenty-first century?

CHAPTER 5

ADAPTATION, INTERPRETATION, AND INFLUENCE

It has been noted often that James was continually frustrated by his attempts to have plays that would achieve popular and critical success in London theaters. It was certainly not for lack of effort and study on his part, and he was a lifelong theatergoer and defender of the new social drama, especially the work of Henrik Ibsen (James heard the first readings of Ibsen while the translators were still drafting the work; see Egan 1972). His social circles included the playwrights, producers, dramatic translators, and leading actors of his time. While his full concentration turned away from theater after the 1895 failure of his *Guy Domville*, he continued to write plays (some of which were produced), and believed that he had learned from his dramatic toil how to construct scenes and provide exposition through dialogue, and to create maximum intensity of effect with minimal means. It might surprise readers of his subtle and complex later fiction that James felt the lessons he had learned from the stage could alter his prose for the better, or how much his work is overlaid elements of the now much-maligned Victorian melodramas. This is so much the case that Peter Brooks, in *The Melodramatic Imagination* (1976), finds this genre's "mode of excess" central to James's work and thinking. We might note that some of James's plays he had adapted from his own fiction and "The Covering End," the other published with *The Turn of the Screw* in *The Two Magics*, apparently began as a play and was converted into a short story.

We might preliminarily consider some of the problems in adapting works of fiction into any other medium, whether for theater, films, or opera. If reading can be a seemingly private engagement between the reader and the text, we know that it is more complex than it first appears. The text is never free of context (where it appears, a popular magazine or a scholarly, annotated edition surrounded by commentary, read in a course or read at the discretion of the reader). The reader is reading at a particular moment and place (and the reading experience is temporal and so this varies even in any one reading) and is influenced by all other cultural information and previously reading, and by the way the reader anticipates and remembers textual information and puts it together in formulating what becomes "the reading." We won't complicate this further by discussing multiple rereadings that revise earlier understandings.

If the private reading is complex, the difficulties of adaptations of fiction have many additional layers and agents. For one thing, the adaptation is often judged by how well it "matches" the private reading experience, including the way characters and setting imagined by readers, all different, are now physically represented by actors and objects on stage or on film. The adaptation may have been expanded by material that the author did not place in the text: added dialogue, added characters, entire scenes or exposition. More likely, especially in the case of novels, much that takes place in the work is cut out for reasons of focus, duration, and budget. It does not cost an author additional payroll or construction costs when writing a crowd scene, a battle, or describing an estate with a lake; the author does not have to find horses or Greek statues or Victorian costumes). All of the visual elements of film, such as the differences in camera technology through time, are not controlled by the author; film and television before a certain time is in black and white, after that in color (and the audience must be relied upon to use their experiences in the world to fill in the colors properly, at least in line with their expectations). Film may or may not have music playing and the characters do not hear it; the soundtrack is to support the visual and plot elements for the viewer. One may now view a film privately on a screen in the home or a small handheld device; the environment of the viewing, everything from décor to the presence of outside sounds, and this viewing could be alone or with other people. In the past, viewing film, like viewing a play or hearing a concert, took place in large venues specifically constructed for these activities and involved not only the surrounding audience and reminders of the extrafilm world, but the size of the images on the screen had an impact on the experience. Add to all of this, the fact that the author normally loses all control of what happens to his or her work when it is adapted (especially when the author has been dead for decades before the work is adapted). Vladimir Nabokov's screenplay for his best-selling novel *Lolita*, for example, was rejected by Stanley Kubrick, the film's director (the version Nabokov wrote would have lovingly preserved his wonderful writing and followed his novelistic vision, but it would have been a talky 11-hour film).

Would James have been satisfied with any of the more than one hundred and twenty-five films and ten operas that have been made of his works so far? James in writing fiction just had to please himself and then the editors who published his work; he knew he also had to satisfy the readers because his future earnings were based on his present sales. But theater, film, opera, and other medium for adaptation are collaborative and rely many dozens of specialists working under the directors and producers. Each is involved with interpretation and these will not only vary from each other and from the author, but they will vary through repeated performances or with different casts or singers. While James, in editing and revising the New York Edition, could authorize all of the words of his texts, he could not extend such stability into the future adaptations and the medium and technology he could not foresee. Philip Horne has made an intriguing suggestion.

> If he had been born a few decades earlier, James might have written for film, like Scott Fitzgerald. . . . or like the novelist Hugh Walpole, James's young friend, who went to Hollywood in the 1930s. James . . . took a lively interest in what we now know as the mass media. In 1900 he took his 13-year-old niece to the London Alhambra to a variety show including Biograph films of the Boer War. He wrote to her afterwards hoping "that some of the rather horrid figures and sounds that passed before us at the theater didn't haunt your dreams." They seem to have haunted his. (Horne 2000: 36)

The best recent study on the interaction and development of James in the theater, as well as the best discussion of theatrical adaptations of *The Turn of the Screw*, was published by Frances Babbage (2005). Babbage discusses the theatrical allusions and references throughout the story, such as Peter Quint seen first as an actor or the estate seen as a theater after the play, and questions the notion from Leon Edel and others that James was entirely traumatized by the popular rejection of *Guy Domville* and fled from London theater altogether. This supported Edel's psychoanalytic biographical reading of James as returning to his own childhood and family conflicts in those post-1895 works featuring children and in his memoirs. Babbage wants to draw attention to the work's "elusive qualities of theatricality: to ideas of acting and role-play that produce, for the reader as well as the protagonist, a conflicted sense of what is 'real'; to qualities of shadow and stillness that heighten anticipation and create a focus for action and speech that is shockingly compelling; to the way in which the theatre auditorium itself—a space marked literally and figuratively with the traces of past performance, becomes a powerful and unsettling metaphor through which we can read the haunted scene of Bly" (Babbage 2005: 132).

There are two major theater productions of *The Turn of the Screw*: William Archibald's play titled *The Innocents* (1950) and Jeffrey Hatcher's version (1996) and in some way these recapitulate the critical arguments that have been traced in the earlier chapters. Archibald's work has an overt agenda, announced in the playbill for the original production, of overthrowing the psychoanalytic reading of the work that had come to dominate, at least in academic circles, the perception of the work. That is, that the ghosts do not exist except as hallucinations in the mind of the sexually thwarted governess. In Archibald's version, as Babbage points out, the governess, Mrs. Grose, Miles, Flora, and the audience "all see the ghosts, unmistakably, albeit the appearances of Quint and Jessel are veiled by shadow; there is no suggestion that might be solely a product of neurosis. Archibald's program notes reinforce this, as they sharply criticize the school of interpretive thought led by Edmund Wilson" (Babbage 2005: 144). Specifically, he felt the psychoanalytic approach closed down the viewing of the work as a ghost story. Of course, his own insistence on the reality of the ghosts necessarily closes down the "non-apparitionist" alternative of the hallucinations projected by the governess. Hatcher's version, described frequently by reviewers as minimalist tries to be faithful not to the realistic goal of the suspension of disbelief (supported by the trappings of realism such as convincing set and costumes, appropriate casting of actors to match what will seem to the audience as matching their views of the characters, and so on), but to the ambiguities and indeterminacies of James's work. He has only two actors, a man and a woman. The woman plays the governess and no one else; the man plays the master, Miles, and Mrs. Grose; Miss Jessel and Peter Quint are not represented except by the governess' words, facial expressions, and body language. Flora, too, is only an imagined space with her presence indicated by the other two actors and her "reality," like the ghosts' existence as spirits or as hallucinations, dependent on the actors and the audience. There is no set, there are no props; the stage is just open and dark so that everything is carried by the acting. Babbage notes that "Hatcher's process has been ferocious indeed, pulling out just bare bones: a skeleton, a ghost text that remembers rather than re-enacts James's tale" (Babbage 148). In a way, by trying to remove any ambiguity, Archibald's version is like the tightly controlled traditional Victorian novel in which the reader is always guided along by either the omniscient third-person narrator (with summaries, moral lessons, exposition, and an epilogue in which poetic justice is meted out) or a similarly sympathetic and reliable first-person narrator who similarly keeps a tight rein on the story. In allowing all the unresolved questions and possibilities to remain, and in forcing the audience to imagine the existence of Flora as well as Miss Jessel and Quint or the setting, as well as having to see the multiple characters of both genders played by one actor, Hatcher embraces the post-1970s Derridean, deconstructive reading of the work's permanent undecidability.

In her useful and thorough filmography, J. Sarah Koch lists 16 film or television versions of *The Turn of the Screw* made between 1955 and 2000 (Koch 2002: 351–4). Many of these, especially, those made for television, are not available for viewing but the production notes Koch provides indicates some of these might be particularly interesting. The first television version, shown in 1957 and only 36-minutes long, was adapted for the screen by Gore Vidal. The 1959 NBC production was directed by John Frankenheimer (director of *The Manchurian Candidate* and *Seven Days in May*) and starred Ingrid Bergman (of *Casablanca* and *Notorious*) as the governess; the role earned Bergman an Emmy Award. There are French, British, American, and Spanish or Czech coproductions. One, titled *The Others*, was performed on television only once, live, and presumably is lost in the aether. At least four films have been made of Benjamin Britten's 1954 opera (adaptations of adaptations; since Koch's list was published, another film version appeared in 2005, from BBC/Wales; all of my discussion of the opera will be to this one version).

None of the versions I have been able to view include the frame situation (except in Britten's opera), and they all end almost immediately with the death of Miles (though sometimes with a cluster of images from earlier in the film). Instead of the frame, *The Innocents* begins with a voice-over of the distraught older governess saying she wanted to save the children, not destroy them. The opera begins with Douglas's voice from the frame talking about the governess in a sung voice-over while we see a happy Miss Jessel rushing through misty, autumnal woods, a man striding steadily but seen only from the shoulders down, and Miles perched in a tree looking down or else running through the woods clearly spying or following the other figures (this is repeated very effectively and often in this film but is entirely extratextual). Visual and musical leitmotifs replace verbal repetition. The voice of Flora singing an archaic sounding tune, "O Willow Waly," written for the film and played by Miles on the piano, hummed by Flora, and played on a music box and in the soundtrack, appear throughout *The Innocents*. The 2005 film of the opera repeatedly shows from directly the body of drowned Miss Jessel in the water at the edge of the lake, her skin bluish-white, her eyes steadily open, a smile oddly fixed, her arm bent as if waving in greeting. The casting of the films often conflict with the James text. Those who have read the book and then view *The Innocents* (since order is important in interpretation) would see that Deborah Kerr, at 40, was twice as old the governess in the novel, yet she says in her interview with the master this is her first job. The viewer in 1961 would know her as a major star who played a succession of repressed, tight-laced women (including nuns and governesses). Laurence Raw notes, "Unlike other actresses who had essayed Jamesian roles on film, such as Susan Hayward and Olivia de Havilland, Kerr's star image was not that of a strong-willed person but rather an English rose whose demure exterior concealed a passionate nature" (Raw 2006: 63). That is, she already embodied ambiguity and hidden or controlled sexuality. Until the most recent film versions, the governess and the children are older than in the book. To change the 8-year-old Flora and the 10-year-old Miles into teenagers or to apparently remove the age difference between them, alters the immediate perception from the text of their angelic innocence, their presexual purity (in the pre-Freudian, Victorian understanding of children). In the 1974 *The Turn of the Screw* directed by Dan Curtis, Miles is said to be 14, looks at least 16, is twice the size of Flora and is much taller than the governess (played by Lynn Redgrave, looking, with her pastel colors and parasol, like a lost and hurt Mary Poppins). Sometimes the children's wickedness is shown by making them sadistic. In the film just mentioned, the governess finds Miles sitting on a bench and talking to himself about the oneness of nature and sensing the spirit of trees and plants and all animals. When he stands we see, though the governess does not, there is a dead bird left on the bench (this is perhaps based on a shot in *The Innocents* in which Miles has a dead pigeon under his pillow with its neck broken). He enjoys "drowning" ants in water and then laying them in rows on a stone in the sun to watch them come back to life; he blinds a frog to spare it from seeing misery. He was involved in hurting the son of the stableman by pushing him out of the hayloft and just missing impaling him on a pitchfork, said by Mrs. Grose to be an accident but the stableman is certain it was on purpose. It is perhaps not surprising that his favorite bedtime reading is a book about Vlad the Impaler (the director had made his reputation with the popular vampire television series *Dark Shadows*).

The films provide various extra information about Miss Jessel and Peter Quint that had been left in the text only as inferences and dark hints in the governess' conversations with Mrs. Grose. In *The Innocents*, Mrs. Grose gives a great deal more. She says that Quint had his fatal fall immediately behind the house and that Miles found his body and was screaming in horror; she says Quint's eyes were open and he had a look of "surprise, like a fox" hunted down. Miss Jessel had been helplessly in love with Quint although he savagely beat her and knocked her to the floor; she says the pair freely used "rooms in the bright daylight as if they were dark woods" and this may have all been witnessed by Miles and Flora. She says that after Quint's death, Miss Jessel committed suicide. In the 1974 film, the governess finds a stash of letters from Miss Jessel to Quint that she studies through the night, finding them "shocking and shameless." Divulging the details to Mrs. Grose (but not the viewer since this was a television production), the governess concludes that Miles and Flora were present to see the "foul union" and "scenes of lust" between Quint and Miss Jessel. Mrs. Grose tells her Miss Jessel took a room in the village inn and shot herself. The 1999 BBC production begins with a shot of Miss Jessel jumping off a bridge to drown herself. The quite awful film directed by Michael Winner and starring Marlon Brando as Quint, *The Nightcomers* (1971), is entirely a "prequel" showing how evil Miss Jessel and Quint were while they were alive (mainly by having a sadomasochistic relationship, explicitly shown). They were spied on by Miles who then practiced such tying up and undressing with poor Flora (see Raw 2006: chapter 6). The children become so advanced in wickedness they cause the seemingly accidental deaths of both Miss Jessel and Quint.

Of the sixteen films, the one that has received the greatest amount of critical attention and general approval is *The Innocents* (1961), directed by Jack Clayton and starring Deborah Kerr as the governess (unnamed in the text, she is called Miss Giddens in the film). It is based on the play by William Archibald but the screenplay went through many drafts and changes with other writers (including Truman Capote). While Archibald felt his play made it clear that the ghosts were real and the governess was protecting the children from evil influences, the film version has been praised by critics for pre-serving the ambiguity and uncertainties the reader finds in the text, even adding unresolved questions (see Palmer 1977: 213–14; Raw 2006: 57; Recchia 1987: 34). According to Laurence Raw,

> the screenplay includes a sequence that apparently resolves those uncertainties, as Miss Giddens reflects on her time at Bly and speculates on the relationships, past and present, among the chil-dren, Miss Jessel, and Quint. It comprises a montage of images superimposed over her reclining figure—the cracked photograph of Quint, Quint on the tower, Flora's hand holding her pet tortoise, a musical box trilling "O Willow Waly." The dream ends with Miss Giddens imagining how the children have been possessed by the ghosts, with Miss Jessel . . . dancing in silhouette with Flora, Quint putting a possessive arm around Miles's shoulder, and Miss Giddens herself praying for deliverance to the sound of a chiming clock. (2006: 60–1)

This planned scene was not included in the finished film, which ends almost immediately with the death of Miles, as in the book. This pressure to fill in all of the narrative gaps that had been sown through the text is great but however it came about in the revisions and cut-ting, *The Innocents* retains its enigmas. The first-person narrative is impossible to capture fully on film even with the awkwardness of voice-overs for the character's narration or description of his or her reactions or simply providing exposition and links between scenes (the constant voice-over is one of the chief irritations of watching the 1974 film). The camera could be, as they say, subjective, following the experiences and perspective of the protagonist. But this is only seemingly subjective since the camera is watching the protagonist at different distances, framed with the windows or gothic arches of the gazebo or parapet, entering into dark hallways, or looking at the ghosts (and showing them there even if all of the characters other than the protagonist seem not to see them). This gives an objective reality, an omniscient and disinterested perspective, that supports the existence of the ghosts and therefore the sanity of the governess. But this is countered by other techniques. Anthony J. Mazzella traces the conflicting camera angles and information throughout the film, noting "its oscillation of subjective shots undercut by objectified data" (Mazzella 2002: 22). The viewer (and the governess) is kept disoriented and unsettled. Similarly, Clair Hughes finds that,

> From the start we are made uncertain of the data we are given and the images we encounter. Are they the governess's subjective reality or is the camera another "eye," undercutting what she sees and implying alternative realities? . . . Clayton retains James's ambiguity over the ghosts' existence first by fragmenting or blur-ring sightings of them, but most effectively, by making the gover-ness's reactions to what she sees his focus. (2007: 161)

The film is surprising in its variations from verisimilitude. Not only is the black and white often in high contrast, but the enormity of the set (there seem to be at least seven stories to both the house and the tower), but the edges of the film's frames were filtered to be black and muted gray. Clair Hughes notes that "James's first-person narra-tive never reveals what the governess wears, and one wonders if some arrangement had been made with the makers of *The King and I* to re-cycle Kerr's costumes" (Hughes 2007: 161). The statues in the courtyard seem to have heads removed, the rain and thunderstorms regularly pound Bly and blow the windows open. The sound effects are exaggerated; when she first sees Quint on the tower, suddenly all of the birds and winds are silenced. The sexual tension between the governess and Miles grows steadily and this is objectified by showing Miles wildly riding on a galloping horse while there is a new roar of wind and birds that frighten her and make her stagger. During a game of hide and seek, Miles pounces on the governess and "playfully" starts to choke her until she is clearly terrified (and this connects with Mrs. Grose's description of Quint's savage treatment of Miss Jessel). She hears screams, echoes, laughter, and voices (including a woman's voice saying "You are hurting me!"). Most startling to the governess (and probably for viewers), is when Miles asks for a kiss good night. He sits up energetically and presses his lips against hers in a clearly erotic and extended manner. She looks shocked but the scene ends in silence; she does not pull back or object. We have said that the film ends "almost immediately with the death of Miles." But there is one more moment that is shown that may be shocking even for a contemporary audience. After she realizes Miles is dead, she raises him in her arms and kisses him on the lips as the film suddenly ends.

In many ways, the opera version (as shown in the 2005 BBC/Wales film directed by Katie Mitchell with the City of London Sinfonia) is the most successful adaptation, perhaps because of the lack of realism inherent in the genre. Benjamin Britten's 1954 opera, with a libretto by Myfanwy Piper Evans, was created as a chamber opera for performance on a concert stage with singers taking several parts and standing facing the audience. The film, then, is much further adaptation; it retains Britten's music and Piper's words but has it acted out in a brilliantly photographed landscape in period costume; visually, in fact, it is the most appealing and appropriate color version, even while taking additional liberties with the text. It is set in just a few days instead of five months, it is moved from summer and fall to just prior to Christmas, and every scene is shot with golden, orange, and mellow brown autumnal colors, though the interior light, from candles or entering through the windows, is cold, blue (like the repeated image of the corpse of drowned Miss Jessel). The musical motifs are based on a Turn theme and a Screw theme, tightening and loosening, twisting, rising, and falling. The governess' musical "voice" is shared by Quint as they battle over Miles; Flora is always deeply connected with Miss Jessel whose "voice" has a deeper and more somber timbre than the high-pitches and faster music for Quint (an excellent analysis of the music and how Britten developed his ideas and worked with the librettist may be found in Rupprecht 2001). In the film, we see not only memories and dreams in the minds of the various characters, something that could not take place in the first-person narrative, but whole scenes without the presence of governess. Startlingly, Miles' memories include bright summer days with his mother (and this reminds us that she is never mentioned at all in James's work). He is in bed having his mother stroke his head or running to hug her and give her flowers (repeatedly the present action shows the children bringing flowers to the grave of Miss Jessel). The children are often frenetically active (roller-skating through the almost empty house with bare floors and walls, suddenly more convincing than the overly lush opulence of the other films, climbing trees, chasing each other through the woods and in the cemetery); they take the stout governess on a running tour of the house and grounds the moment she arrives at Bly and Miles even dreams of running through the woods or to the tower.

Instead of the scene in James's text where Flora is playing by the lake and makes a toy boat just before the appearance of Miss Jessel, in this work Flora has a female doll dressed in black mourning as Miss Jessel, also dressed in black appears across the lake from her. Flora lowers the doll into the water singing the entire time about sleeping and finding rest. After Flora and the governess leave, Miss Jessel walks to where Flora had been, retrieves the doll from the water, and lies down on her side on a bench, embracing the doll. There is an overhead shot and we see Flora return, take the doll from Miss Jessel and they hold hands. She takes the doll and we later see her smiling silently with Miles who watches as she washes the doll in a basin. The most surreal added scene shows Miles sleeping and a large male hand touches his forehead and wakes and walks upstairs to the top floor. We see a female hand placed on the sleeping Flora and also wakes and goes upstairs. Near the attic a hallway is filled with dozens of candles in glasses floating on water; she walks through this pathway to follow Miles to the parapet. Miles seems about to step off the edge when the governess rushes up and stops him and he says, "You see, I am bad." We later see a scene with Quint leaning over Miss Jessel and caressing her and Miss Jessel suddenly is transformed into her successor, the present governess. Where the meeting of Miss Jessel and the governess in the classroom is wordless and makes the governess feel she is the usurper, in this version the governess is furious to see the woman has entered her kingdom and is using her implements (pens, chalk), and she won't bear it. They have a physical confrontation in which the governess is forced back against the wall and Miss Jessel touches her shoulder. The final confession scene adds to the ending of the other works. While Quint sings, "Don't betray us, Miles!" Miles clearly sees Quint and backs away from him. When Miles says the name "Peter Quint," Quint fades away while singing, with a lilting chant, "I must go." The smiling governess holds the dead Miles. Suddenly there is cut to scenes of Miles and Flora running happily through the woods and graveyard. The governess steps out of the house closing the door behind her, leaving Miles collapsed on the floor. We see a cut of Miles looking down, apparently spying, from the branch of a tree, and the film ends.

In addition to film and opera, *The Turn of the Screw* has been variously taken up by writers of fiction and either expanded or given a prequel, sequel, or different narrative point of view; these are most fully discussed in Adeline Tintner's *Henry James's Legacy: The Afterlife of His Figure and Fiction* (1998: 371–82). Tintner presents the parallels or extensions of *The Turn of the Screw* in novels such as Frances Hodgson Burnett's *The Secret Garden* (1911), Rumer Godden's *The Peacock Spring* (1975), Peter Straub's *Ghost Story* (1979), and Hilary Bailey's *Miles and Flora: A Sequel to Henry James's The Turn of the Screw* (1997; see also Boehm 1998), as well as two short stories: Elizabeth Taylor's "Poor Girl" (1951), and Joyce Carol Oates's "Accursed Inhabitants of the House of Bly" (1994). Since Tintner's book, there has also been Toby Litt's novel *Ghost Story* (2004), as well as six recent novels based on Henry James's life and writings, blurring the boundaries of genre and characters with "real life."

It is impossible to trace the influence of *The Turn of the Screw* because it has permeated two strands following the bifurcation of interpretation: the genres of ghost story, horror story, horror films, on the one hand, and works focused on insanity, depression, parental neglect and relationships between parents and children. Along with Freudian concepts, *The Turn of the Screw* has filtered into the *Zeitgeist* and even people who haven't read it or haven't seen any of the many films or other adaptations, have experienced it second or third hand.

QUESTIONS

1. Imagine you were asked to adapt *The Turn of the Screw* for film, theater, or some other form. What changes from the text do you see you will have to make for this other form? Why?

2. Read three of the works of fiction mentioned in this chapter that extend or respond to James's work. How do they make you reconsider the original?
3. Watch any three film or theatrical adaptations of *The Turn of the Screw*. What is the impact of the different works' visual elements (photography, casting, setting and costumes, etc.)?

CHAPTER 6

GUIDE TO FURTHER READING

SELECTED EDITIONS OF THE PRIMARY TEXT

Henry James, *Complete Stories 1892–1898*. New York: Library of America, 1996. "The Turn of the Screw," 635–740. One of the many volumes in the Library of America collecting James's works, this has the special advantage of printing all of the stories in chronological order so that one may see the development and changes in James's short fiction during the years immediately before he wrote *The Turn of the Screw*.

———, *The Novels and Tales of Henry James*, The New York Edition, vol. 12 (*The Aspern Papers, The Turn of the Screw, The Liar*, and *The Two Faces*). London: Macmillan; New York: Charles Scribner's Sons, 1908. This is the textual source for all subsequent editions of *The Turn of the Screw*. It includes James's Preface to the volume.

———, *The Turn of the Screw*. A Norton Critical Edition, second edition. Deborah Esch and Jonathan Warren, eds. New York: W. W. Norton, 1999. This edition reprints a number of articles and reviews, as well as letters and other documents. The full text of *The Turn of the Screw* appears with many useful footnotes.

———, *The Turn of the Screw*. Case Studies in Contemporary Criticism, second edition. Peter G. Beidler, ed. Boston and New York: Bedford/St. Martin's, 2004. This edition reprints and annotates the text and provides a large selection of documents providing biographical and cultural context, a summary of criticism, and applications of five different current critical approaches to the work specifically commissioned for the volume, along with brief introductions to the methods.

———, *The Turn of the Screw and Other Stories*. T. J. Lustig, ed. Oxford World Classics. Oxford and New York: Oxford University Press, 1992, reissued, 2008. This includes other major ghost stories by James and so emphasizes that continued thread running through his work.

GENERAL

There are hundreds of books on James. Fogel, Freedman, Gale, and Rawlings are recent attempts to provide critical overviews and original articles on a wide range of topics. The topics covered and the length of the articles vary from one work to the next but they are all useful.

Fogel, Daniel Mark, ed. *A Companion to Henry James Studies*. Westport, CT: Greenwood, 1993.

Freedman, Jonathan, ed. *The Cambridge Companion to Henry James*. Cambridge: Cambridge University Press, 1998.

Gale, Robert L. *A Henry James Encyclopedia*. New York: Greenwood, 1989.

Heller, Terry. *The Turn of the Screw: Bewildered Vision*. Boston: Twayne, 1989. The most comprehensive book-length work specifically on *The Turn of the Screw* with coverage of criticism through the mid-1980s.

Rawlings, Peter, ed. *Palgrave Advances in Henry James Studies*. New York: Palgrave Macmillan, 2007.

Reed, Kimberly C. and Peter G. Beidler, eds. *Approaches to Teaching Henry James's* Daisy Miller *and* The Turn of the Screw. New York: Modern Language Association, 2005. Not for students but useful brief articles on a variety of ways to teach *Turn of the Screw* in various college classroom contexts and offering a range of approaches.

CHAPTER 1 CONTEXTS

For some of the literary movements and societal contexts for this period of James's work and *The Turn of the Screw* in particular, see the works on Victorian literature (Davis), Decadence and the Fin-de-siècle (Constable, et al., and Ledger and Luckhurst), modernism (Childs, Stevenson, and Trotter), and the Edwardian period (Rose). On James and the supernatural (his ghost stories, the work of the Society for Psychical Research, life after death), see the studies by Banta, Beidler, Hutchinson, Lustig, Thurschwell, and Tursi. For biographies of James, see Edel, Graham, Kaplan, and Novick (1996 and 2007). Lewis's work is an unusual "group biography" of the entire James family. For a selection from James's notebooks, see Edel and Powers. On James's letters, see Edel's four-volume selection, Horne's innovative life-told-in-letters, Moore for the correspondence with Edmund Gosse, and Skrupskelis and Berkeley for a selection of both sides of the correspondence between James and his brother William. The first complete edition of James's letters just started publication in 2006 and will take many years and volumes; on this, see Walker (2000) and Walker and Zacharias (2006, 2007); also see Crane. On the New York Edition, see McWhirter. The volumes of James's literary essays provide innumerable insights into his influences and aesthetics; his nonliterary essays were collected by Walker (1999).

Banta, Martha. *Henry James and the Occult*. Bloomington, IN: Indiana University Press, 1972.

Beidler, Peter G. *Ghosts, Demons, and Henry James: The Turn of the Screw at the Turn of the Century*. Columbia, MO: University of Missouri Press, 1989.

Childs, Peter. *Modernism*. London: Routledge, 2000.

Constable, Liz, Dennis Denisoff, and Matthew Potolsky, eds. *Perennial Decay: On the Aesthetics & Politics of Decadence*. Philadelphia, PA: University of Pennsylvania Press, 1999.

Crane, Brian. "From Family Papers to Archive: The James Letters." *Henry James Review* 29 (2008), 144–62.

Davis, Philip. *The Victorians*. 1830–1880. Vol. 8 of the Oxford English Literary History. Oxford: Oxford University Press, 2002.

Edel, Leon. *Henry James: A Life*. New York: Harper & Row, 1985.

———, ed. *Henry James Letters*, 4 vols. Cambridge, MA: Harvard University Press, 1974–1984.

———. *The Life of Henry James*, 5 vols. Philadelphia, PA: J. B. Lippincott, 1953–1972.

Edel, Leon and Lyall H. Powers, eds. *The Complete Notebooks of Henry James*. New York: Oxford University Press, 1987.

Graham, Kenneth. *Henry James: A Literary Life*. New York: St. Martin's Press, 1999.

Gunter, Susan E. and Steven H. Jobe, eds. *Dearly Beloved Friends: Henry James's Letters to Younger Men*. Ann Arbor, MI: University of Michigan Press, 2001.

Horne, Philip, ed. *Henry James: A Life in Letters*. New York: Penguin Books, 1999.

Hutchison, Hazel. *Seeing and Believing: Henry James and the Spiritual World*. New York: Palgrave Macmillan, 2006.

James, Henry. *Essays on Literature, American Writers, English Writers*. New York: Library of America, 1984.

———. *French Writers, Other European Writers & The Prefaces to the New York Edition*. New York: Library of America, 1984.

Kaplan, Fred. *Henry James: The Imagination of Genius: A Biography*. New York: William Morrow, 1992.

Ledger, Sally and Roger Luckhurst, eds. *The Fin de Siècle: A Reader in Cultural History c. 1880–1900*. Oxford: Oxford University Press, 2000.

Lewis, R. W. B. *The Jameses: A Family Narrative*. New York: Farrar, Straus, and Giroux, 1991.

Lustig, T. J. *Henry James and the Ghostly*. Cambridge: Cambridge University Press, 1994.

McWhirter, David, ed. *Henry James's New York Edition: The Construction of Authorship*. Stanford: Stanford University Press, 1999.

Moore, Rayburn S., ed. *Selected Letters of Henry James to Edmund Gosse, 1882–1915*. Baton Rouge, LA: Louisiana State University Press, 1988.

Novick, Sheldon M. *Henry James: The Young Master*. New York: Random House, 1996.

———. *Henry James: The Mature Master*. New York: Random House, 2007.

Rose, Jonathan. *The Edwardian Temperament 1895–1919*. Athens, OH: Ohio University Press, 1986.

Skrupskelis, Ignas K. and Elizabeth M. Berkeley, eds. *William and Henry James: Selected Letters*. Charlottesville, VA: University Press of Virginia, 1997.

Stevenson, Randall. *Modernist Fiction*. Lexington, KY: University Press of Kentucky, 1992.

Thurschwell, Pamela. *Literature, Technology and Magical Thinking, 1880–1920*. Cambridge: Cambridge University Press, 2001.

Trotter, David. "The Modernist Novel." In Michael Levenson, ed., *The Cambridge Companion to Modernism*. Cambridge: Cambridge University Press, 1999, 70–99.

Tursi, Renée. "Henry James's Self-Reiterating Habit in 'Is There a Life after Death?'" *Henry James Review* 23 (2002), 176–95.

Walker, Pierre A., ed. *Henry James on Culture: Collected Essays on Politics and the American Social Scene*. Lincoln, NE: University of Nebraska Press, 1999.

———. "Leon Edel and the 'Policing' of the James Letters." *Henry James Review* 21 (2000), 279–89.

Walker, Pierre A. and Greg W. Zacharias. *The Complete Letters of Henry James, 1855–1872: Volumes 1 and 2*. Lincoln, NE: University of Nebraska Press, 2006. This project will displace all of the other specialized or selected editions of James's correspondence.

———. "Editing *The Complete Letters of Henry James*." In Peter Rawlings, ed., *Palgrave Advances in Henry James Studies*. New York: Palgrave Macmillan, 2007, 239–62.

CHAPTER 2 LANGUAGE, STYLE, AND FORM

Ironically, many studies of writers' style are dry and technical. However, once the reader learns the vocabulary and variety of methods within style studies, or the studies of specific narrative techniques, these provide great rewards, drawing attention to what the reader might have experienced but could not articulate and so could not convey. The works on style in James include Chatman, Cross, Dry, Isle, Kurnick, Norrman, Ohi, Smit, Veeder (1975), and Teahan. These are not focused on *The Turn of the Screw* specifically but on James's experimental and late style generally. The works on narrative techniques in *The Turn of the Screw*, especially the frame story, narrators, and title, include Álvarez Amorós, Beidler, Kafalenos, Sawyer, and Williams. On illustrations in the magazine publication, see Cappello and Sonstegard. There are many studies relating *The Turn of the Screw* to fairy tales, ghost stories, and the literary tradition of the Gothic. See Auchard, Burkholder-Mosco and Carse, Butterworth-McDermott, Chinitz, Coulson, Jang, Lewis, Schleifer, Sheppard, and Veeder (1999).

Álvarez Amorós, José Antonio. "Possible-World Semantics, Frame Text, Insert Text, and Unreliable Narration: The Case of *The Turn of the Screw*." *Style* 25.1 (1991), 42–70.

Auchard, John. *Silence in Henry James: The Heritage in Symbolism and Decadence.* University Park, PA: Pennsylvania State University Press, 1986.

Beidler, Paul G. *Frames in James:* The Tragic Mus′, The Turn of the Screw, What Maisie Knew, *and* The Ambassadors. V.ctoria, BC: University of Victoria ELS Monograph Series, 1993. Useıul for its description of a variety of framing techniques in James's fiction.

Burkholder-Mosco, Nicole and Wendy Carse. "'Wondrous Material to Play On': Children as Sites of Gothic Liminality in *The Turn of the Screw, The Innocents,* and *The Others.*" *Studies in the Humanities* 32.2 (Dec., 2005), 201–20.

Butterworth-McDermott, Christine. "James's Fractured Fairy-Tale: How the Governess Gets Grimm." *Henry James Review* 28 (2007), 43–56.

Cameron, Sharon. *Thinking in Henry James.* Chicago: University of Chicago Press, 1989.

Cappello, Mary. "Governing the Master('s) Plot: Frames of Desire in Demuth and James." *Word & Image* 8.2 (April–June, 1992), 154–70.

Chatman, Seymour. *The Later Style of Henry James.* Oxford: Basil Blackwell, 1972.

Chinitz, Lisa G. "Fairy Tale Turned Ghost Story: James's *The Turn of the Screw.*" *Henry James Review* 15.3 (Fall, 1994), 264–85.

Coulson, Victoria. "Prisons, Palaces, and the Architecture of the Imagination." In Peter Rawlings, ed., *Palgrave Advances in Henry James Studies.* New York: Palgrave Macmillan, 2007, 169–92.

Cross, Mary. *Henry James: The Contingencies of Style.* New York: St. Martin's Press, 1993.

Dry, Helen Aristar. "Ghostly Ambiguity: Presuppositional Constructions in *The Turn of the Screw.*" *Style* 25.1 (Spring, 1991), 71–88.

Graham, Wendy. "Pictures for Texts." *Henry James Review* 24.1 (Winter, 2003), 1–26.

Ian, Marcia. "Henry James and the Spectacle of Loss: Psychoanalytic Metaphysics." In Sally Ledger and Scott McCracken, eds. *Cultural Politics at the Fin de Siecle.* Cambridge: Cambridge University Press, 1995, 115–36.

Isle, Walter. *Experiments in Form: Henry James's Novels, 1896–1901.* Cambridge, MA: Harvard University Press, 1968.

Jang, Kiyoon. "Governess as Ghostwriter: Unauthorized Authority and Uncanny Authorship in Henry James's 'The Turn of the Screw.'" *Henry James Review* 28 (2007), 13–25.

Kafalenos, Emma. "Not (Yet) Knowing: Epistemological Effects of Deferred and Suppressed Information in Narrative." In David Herman, ed., *Narratologies: New Perspectives on Narrative Analysis.* Columbus, OH: Ohio State University Press, 1999, 33–65.

Kurnick, David. "What Does Jamesian Style Want?" *Henry James Review* 28 (2007), 213–22.

Lewis, Pericles. "'The Reality of the Unseen': Shared Fictions and Religious Experience in the Ghost Stories of Henry James." *Arizona Quarterly* 61.2 (Summer, 2005), 33–66.

Miller, J. Hillis. "The 'Quasi-Turn-of-the-Screw Effect': How to Raise a Ghost with Words." *Oxford Literary Review* 25 (2003), 121–37.

Norrman, Ralf. *The Insecure World of Henry James's Fiction: Intensity and Ambiguity*. New York: St. Martin's Press, 1982.

Ohi, Kevin. "'The Author of Beltraffio': The Exquisite Boy and Henry James's Equivocal Aestheticism." *ELH* 72 (2005), 747–67.

———. "Belatedness and Style." In Peter Rawlings, ed., *Palgrave Advances in Henry James Studies*. New York: Palgrave Macmillan, 2007, 126–46.

———. "'The novel is older, and so are the young': On the Queerness of Style." *Henry James Review* 27 (2006), 140–55.

Sawyer, Richard. "'What's your title?' *The Turn of the Screw*." *Studies in Short Fiction* 30 (1993), 53–61.

Schleifer, Ronald. "The Trap of the Imagination: The Gothic Tradition, Fiction, and *The Turn of the Screw*." In Neil Cornwell and Maggie Malone, eds., *The Turn of the Screw and What Maisie Knew*. New York: St. Martin's, 1998, 19–41.

Sheppard, E. A. *Henry James and* The Turn of the Screw. Suffolk, VA: Auckland University Press/Oxford University Press, 1974.

Smit, David W. *The Language of a Master: Theories of Style and the Late Writing of Henry James*. Carbondale, IL: Southern Illinois University Press, 1988.

Sonstegard, Adam. "'A Merely Pictorial Subject': *The Turn of the Screw*." *Studies in American Fiction* 33.1 (Spring, 2005), 59–85.

Teahan, Sheila. "The Literal Turn of the Figurative Screw." *Arizona Quarterly* 62.3 (Autumn, 2006), 63–82.

Veeder, William. *Henry James—The Lessons of the Master: Popular Fiction and Personal Style in the Nineteenth Century*. Chicago: University of Chicago Press, 1975.

———. "The Nurturance of the Gothic: *The Turn of the Screw*." *Gothic Studies* 1.1 (Aug., 1999), 47–85.

Williams, Jeff. "Narrative Games: The Frame of *The Turn of the Screw*." *Journal of Narrative Technique* 28.1 (Winter, 1998), 43–55.

CHAPTER 3 READING *THE TURN OF THE SCREW*

There is overlap in the works in this section. The same article or book may discuss gender, the homophobia of the late 1890s and how it can be seen through James's text, or about how children were understood and represented. For those interested in gender studies and feminist approaches, see Bell, DeKoven, Kauffman, McWhirter, and Newman. Works focused on gay studies or queer studies or the impact of the Oscar Wilde trial, see Fletcher, Matheson, McCormack, Mendelssohn, Savoy, Smith, and Soltysik. Matheson and Mendelssohn are perhaps the best points-of-departure. On the study of other extratextual contexts (such as governess fiction, the child study movement, or the representation of children in James's fiction), see Glazener, Killoran, Levander, Losano, Pagan, Pearson, Shine, and Thormann. On hysteria, see Mahbobah, Renner, Rivkin, and Wagenknecht (particularly useful for Freud's case history on hysteria, "Dora," and its parallels to James's work and thinking). Van Peer and van der Kamp have recently published a comprehensive survey of the incompatible readings of *The Turn of the Screw.*

Bell, Millicent. "Class, Sex, and the Victorian Governess: James's *The Turn of the Screw.*" In Vivian R. Pollak, ed., *New Essays on Daisy Miller and The Turn of the Screw.* New York: Cambridge University Press, 1993, 91–119.

DeKoven, Marianne. "A Different Story: 'The Yellow Wallpaper' and *The Turn of the Screw,*" chapter two of her volume *Rich and Strange: Gender, History, Modernism.* Princeton: Princeton University Press, 1991, 38–63. Compelling essay bringing together *The Turn of the Screw* with a contemporaneous work by Charlotte Perkins Gilman, raising the issues about hysteria and gender roles.

Flatley, Jonathan. "Reading into Henry James." *Criticism* 46.1 (Winter, 2004), 103–23.

Fletcher, John. "The Haunted Closet: Henry James's Queer Spectrality." *Textual Practice* 14.1 (2000), 53–80.

Glazener, Nancy. "Romances for 'Big and Little Boys': The U.S. Romantic Revival of the 1890s and James's *The Turn of the Screw.*" In Deirdre Lynch and William B. Warner, eds., *Cultural Institutions of the Novel.* Durham, NC: Duke University Press, 1996, 369–98.

Kauffman, Linda S. *Discourses of Desire: Gender, Genre, and Epistolary Fictions.* Ithaca, NY: Cornell University Press, 1986.

Killoran, Helen. "The Governess, Mrs. Grose and 'the Poison of an Influence' in *The Turn of the Screw.*" *Modern Language Studies* 23.2 (Spring, 1993), 13–24.

Levander, Caroline. "'Informed yes': The 1890s Child Study Movement and Henry James's *The Turn of the Screw.*" *Critical Matrix* 12.1–2 (Fall, 2000–Spring, 2001), 8–25.

Losano, Antonia. "*East Lynn, The Turn of the Screw,* and the Female Doppelgänger in Governess Fiction." *Nineteenth Century Studies* 18 (2004), 99–116.

Ludwig, Sämi. "Metaphors, Cognition and Behavior: The Reality of Sexual Puns in *The Turn of the Screw.*" *Mosaic* 27.1 (Mar., 1994), 33–53.

Mahbobah, Albaraq. "Hysteria, Rhetoric, and the Politics of Reversal in Henry James's *The Turn of the Screw.*" *Henry James Review* 17.2 (1996), 149–61.

Matheson, Neill. "Talking Horrors: James, Euphemism, and the Specter of Wilde." *American Literature* 71.4 (Dec., 1999), 709–50.

McCormack, Peggy, ed. *Questioning the Master: Gender and Sexuality in Henry James's Writings.* Newark, NJ: University of Delaware Press, 2000.

McWhirter, David. "In the 'Other House' of Fiction: Writing, Authority, and Femininity in *The Turn of the Screw.*" In Vivian R. Pollak, ed., *New Essays on Daisy Miller and The Turn of the Screw.* New York: Cambridge University Press, 1993, 121–48.

Newman, Beth. "Getting Fixed: Feminine Identity and Scopic Crisis in 'The Turn of the Screw.'" *Novel* 26.1 (Fall, 1992), 43–63.

Nikolopoulou, Kalliopi. "Autospectrography: On Henry James's *The Turn of the Screw*." *Journal of Modern Literature* 28.1 (Fall, 2004), 1–24.

Pagan, Nicholas O. "Henry James's Children and the Gift of Friendship." *Philological Quarterly* 83.3 (Summer, 2004), 275–96.

Pearson, John H. "Repetition and Subversion in Henry James's *The Turn of the Screw*." In Neil Cornwell and Maggie Malone, eds., *The Turn of the Screw and What Maisie Knew*. New York: St. Martin's, 1998, 79–99.

Pearson, Maeve. "Re-exposing the Jamesian Child: The Paradox of Children's Privacy." *Henry James Review* 28 (2007), 101–19.

Peer, Willie van and Ewout van der Kamp. "(In)compatible Interpretations? Contesting Readings of 'The Turn of the Screw.'" *MLN* 110.4 (Sept., 1995), 692–710.

Pittock, Malcolm. "The Decadence of *The Turn of the Screw*." *Essays in Criticism* 55.4 (2005), 332–51.

Posnock, Ross. *The Trial of Curiosity: Henry James, William James, and the Challenge of Modernity.* New York: Oxford University Press, 1991.

Reed, Kimberley C. "'The Hideous Obscure': Historical Backgrounds of *The Turn of the Screw*," in Reed and Beidler (2005), 39–45.

Renaux, Sigrid. *The Turn of the Screw: A Semiotic Reading.* New York: Peter Lang, 1993.

Renner, Stanley. "'Red hair, very red, close-curling': Sexual Hysteria, Physiognomical Bogeymen, and the 'Ghosts' in *The Turn of the Screw*." In Peter G. Beidler, ed., *The Turn of the Screw*, second edition. Boston and New York: Bedford/St. Martin's, 2004, 271–89.

Rivkin, Julie. "The Genius of the Unconscious: Psychoanalytic Criticism." In Peter Rawlings, ed., *Palgrave Advances in Henry James Studies*. New York: Palgrave Macmillan, 2007, 59–79.

Savoy, Eric. "The Jamesian Turn: A Primer on Queer Formalism," in Reed and Beidler (2005), 132–42.

Scofield, Martin. "Implied Stories: Implication, Moral Panic and *The Turn of the Screw*." *Journal of the Short Story in English* 40 (Spring, 2003), 97–107.

Seltzer, Mark. "The Postal Unconscious." *Henry James Review* 21 (2000), 197–206.

Shine, Muriel G. *The Fictional Children of Henry James.* Chapel Hill, NC: University of North Carolina Press, 1968.

Smith, Allan Lloyd. "A Word Kept Back in *The Turn of the Screw*." *Victorian Literature and Culture* 24 (1996), 139–58.

Soltysik, Agnieszka M. "Recovering 'Covering End': What Queer Theory Can Do for *The Turn of the Screw*." *Victorian Literature and Culture* 36 (2008), 247–52.

Sorensen, Sue. "A Visual Approach to *The Turn of the Screw*," in Reed and Beidler (2005), 195–201.

Tambling, Jeremy. "Allegorical Autobiography: *The Turn of the Screw*," chapter five in his volume *Henry James*. New York: St. Martin's Press, 2000, 94–112.

Teahan, Sheila. "'I caught him, yes, I held him': The Ghostly Effects of Reading (in) *The Turn of the Screw*." In Peter G. Beidler, ed., *The Turn of the Screw*, second edition. Boston and New York: Bedford/St. Martin's, 2004, 349–63.

Thormann, Janet. "The Unconscious and the Construction of the Child." *Literature and Psychology* 42.2 (1996), 16–36.

Wagenknecht, David. "Here's Looking at You, Peter Quint: 'The Turn of the Screw,' Freud's 'Dora,' and the Aesthetics of Hysteria." *American Imago* 55.4 (1998), 423–58.

Weisbuch, Robert. "James and the American Sacred." *Henry James Review* 22 (2001), 217–28.

———. "Henry James and the Idea of Evil." In Jonathan Freedman, ed. *The Cambridge Companion to Henry James*. Cambridge: Cambridge University Press, 1998, 102–19.

Wesley, Marilyn C. "The Remembered Future: Neuro-Cognitive Identity in Henry James's *The Turn of the Screw*." *College Literature* 31.2 (Spring, 2004), 80–98.

Yeazell, Ruth Bernard. *Language and Knowledge in the Late Novels of Henry James*. Chicago: University of Chicago Press, 1976.

CHAPTER 4 CRITICAL RECEPTION AND PUBLISHING HISTORY

Histories of the criticism of *The Turn of the Screw*, from the initial serial publication (1898) through the book publication and then its reprinting in the New York Edition (1908), including excerpts from letters to James, book reviews in England and the United States, and then through the changing waves of critical theories of the twentieth century, have been published by Beidler, Duperray (whose focus is Europe), and Hoople. The most important work of psychoanalytic criticism, combining Freud, Lacan, and Derrida, is Felman; also emphasizing the work's ambiguity but from a linguistic and structuralist perspective are the books by Brooke-Rose and Rimmon. Studies of sexuality or homosexuality (and Wilde and aestheticism as essential for understanding the late James) include Freedman, Graham, Haralson, Mendelssohn, Savoy (2007), Sedgwick, and Walton (1992, 2004). On issues of history and class in James, see Buelens and Aijmer, Robbins, Rowe (1984, 2007), and Wilson.

Beidler, Peter G. "A Critical History of *The Turn of the Screw*." In Peter G. Beidler, ed., *The Turn of the Screw*, second edition. Boston and New York: Bedford/St. Martin's, 2004, 189–222.

Brooke-Rose, Christine. *The Rhetoric of the Unreal*. Cambridge: Cambridge University Press, 1981.

———. "The Squirm of the True: Part 1: An Essay in Non-Methodology." *PTL* 1 (1976), 265–94. Part 2: "A Structural Analysis of Henry James's *The Turn of the Screw*." *PTL* 1 (1976), 513–46. Part 3: "Surface Structure in Narrative." *PTL* 2 (1977), 517–62.

Buelens, Gert and Celia Aijmer. "The Sense of the Past: History and Historical Criticism." In Peter Rawlings, ed., *Palgrave Advances in Henry James Studies*. New York: Palgrave Macmillan, 2007, 283–300.

Duperray, Annick, ed. *The Reception of Henry James in Europe*. London: Continuum, 2006.

Felman, Shoshana. "Turning the Screw of Interpretation." In Shoshana Felman, ed., *Literature and Psychoanalysis: The Question of Reading Otherwise*. Baltimore, MD: Johns Hopkins University Press, 1980, 90–207.

Freedman, Jonathan. *Professions of Taste: Henry James, British Aestheticism, and Commodity Culture*. Stanford: Stanford University Press, 1990.

Graham, Wendy. *Henry James's Thwarted Love*. Stanford: Stanford University Press, 1999.

Haralson, Eric. "'His Little Heart Dispossessed': Ritual Sexorcism in *The Turn of the Screw*." In Peggy McCormack, ed., *Questioning the Master: Gender and Sexuality in Henry James's Writing*. Newark, DE: University of Delaware Press, 2000, 133–48.

Hoople, Robin P. *Distinguished Discord: Discontinuity and Pattern in the Critical Tradition of* The Turn of the Screw. Lewisburg, PA: Bucknell University Press, 1997.

McMaster, Graham. "Henry James and India: A Historical Reading of *The Turn of the Screw*." *Clio* 18 (1988), 23–40.

Mendelssohn, Michèle. *Henry James, Oscar Wilde and Aesthetic Culture*. Edinburgh: Edinburgh University Press, 2007.

Rimmon, Shlomith. *The Concept of Ambiguity—the Example of James*. Chicago: University of Chicago Press, 1977.

Robbins, Bruce. "'They don't much count, do they?': The Unfinished History of *The Turn of the Screw*." In Peter G. Beidler, ed., *The Turn of the Screw*, second edition. Boston and New York: Bedford/St. Martin's, 2004, 333–46.

Rowe, John Carlos. "Henry James and Globalization." In Peter Rawlings, ed., *Palgrave Advances in Henry James Studies*. New York: Palgrave Macmillan, 2007, 283–300.

———. *The Theoretical Dimensions of Henry James*. Madison, WI: University of Wisconsin Press, 1984.

Savoy, Eric. "*Entre chien et loup*: Henry James, Queer Theory, and the Biographical Imperative." In Peter Rawlings, ed., *Palgrave Advances in Henry James Studies*. New York: Palgrave Macmillan, 2007, 283–300.

———. "Subjunctive Biography." *Henry James Review* 27 (2006), 248–55.

Sedgwick, Eve Kosofsky. "The Beast in the Closet: James and the Writing of Homosexual Panic." In Ruth Yeazell, ed., *Sex, Politics, and Science in the Nineteenth-Century Novel*. Baltimore, MD: Johns Hopkins University Press, 1985, 148–86.

Stevens, Hugh. *Henry James and Sexuality*. New York: Cambridge University Press, 1998.

Teahan, Sheila. "Mastering Critical Theory." In Peter Rawlings, ed., *Palgrave Advances in Henry James Studies*. New York: Palgrave Macmillan, 2007, 11–34.

Walton, Priscilla. *The Disruption of the Feminine in Henry James*. Toronto: University of Toronto Press, 1992.

———. "'He took no notice of her; he looked at me': Subjectivities and Sexualities in *The Turn of the Screw*." In Peter G. Beidler, ed., *The Turn of the Screw*, second edition. Boston and New York: Bedford/St. Martin's, 2004, 305–16.

Wilson, Robert Andrew. "'And He So Dreadfully Below': Teaching Issues of Social Class in *The Turn of the Screw*," in Reed and Beidler (2005), 53–62.

CHAPTER 5 ADAPTATION, INTERPRETATION, AND INFLUENCE

The impact on James's fiction through his lifelong engagement with the theater and opera is differently treated in the works by Babbage, Brooks, and Egan. Many writers of fiction have either represented James himself as character in their works or else utilized his plots or characters as starting points for their own novels or short stories (on these, see Boehm and Tintner). On the many television and film versions of *The Turn of the Screw*, see Brown (1998, 2005), Deutsch, Horne, Hughes, Koch, Mazella, Palmer, Raw, Recchia, and Wilson. On Benjamin Britten's opera version, scholarly studies that can be understood by nonmusicologists include Clippinger, Halliwell, and Rupprecht.

Babbage, Frances. "The Play of the Surface: Theater and *The Turn of the Screw*." *Comparative Drama* 39.2 (Summer, 2005), 131–56. This is the best study of the theatrical elements within the work, as well as discussing James's experiences in the theater and what effect this had on his fiction; he also discusses theatrical versions of *The Turn of the Screw*.

Boehm, Beth A. "A Postmodern Turn of *The Turn of the Screw*." *Henry James Review* 19.3 (1998), 245–54. On recent novels recasting or augmenting James's work.

Bradley, John R., ed., *Henry James on Stage and Screen*. New York: Palgrave, 2000.

Brooks, Peter. *The Melodramatic Imagination: Balzac, Henry James, Melodrama, and the Mode of Excess*. New Haven, CT: Yale University Press, 1976. A key work for this still easily missed aspect of the seemingly cerebral and controlled James.

Brown, Monika. "Film Music as Sister Art: Adaptations of *The Turn of the Screw*." *Mosaic* 31.1 (Mar., 1998), 61–81.

———. "'A Matter of Appreciation, Speculation, Imagination': Interpreting *The Turn of the Screw* and Film Adaptations," in Reed and Beidler (2005), 186–94.

Clippinger, David. "The Hidden Life: Benjamin Britten's Homoerotic Reading of Henry James's *The Turn of the Screw*." In Michael J. Meyer, ed., *Literature and Musical Adaptation*. Amsterdam: Rodopi, 2002, 137–51.

Deutsch, Michelle. "Ceremonies of Innocence: Boys and Men in *The Turn of the Screw*." In John R. Bradley, ed., *Henry James on Stage and Screen*. New York: Palgrave, 2000, 72–83.

Egan, Michael. *Henry James; The Ibsen Years*. London: Vision Press, 1972.

Halliwell, Michael. "'The Master's Voice': Henry James and Opera." In John R. Bradley, ed., *Henry James on Stage and Screen*. New York: Palgrave, 2000, 23–34.

Horne, Philip. "Henry James: Varieties of Cinematic Experience," in John R. Bradley (2000), 35–55.

Hughes, Clair. "Scene and Screen." In Peter Rawlings, ed., *Palgrave Advances in Henry James Studies*. New York: Palgrave Macmillan, 2007, 147–68.

Koch, J. Sarah. "A Henry James Filmography." In Susan M. Griffin, ed. *Henry James Goes to the Movies*. Lexington, KY: University Press of Kentucky, 2002, 335–57. The fullest filmography (listing and full information about the filmed versions, including made-for-television versions, of James's works), complete to about 2000.

Mazzella, Anthony J. "'The Story . . . Held Us': 'The Turn of the Screw' from Henry James to Jack Clayton." In Susan M. Griffin, ed., *Henry James Goes to the Movies*. Lexington, KY: University Press of Kentucky, 2002, 11–33.

Palmer, James W. "Cinematic Ambiguity: James's 'The Turn of the Screw' and Clayton's *The Innocents*." *Literature Film Quarterly* 5 (1977), 198–215.

Raw, Laurence. *Adapting Henry James to the Screen: Gender, Fiction, and Film*. Lanham, MD: Scarecrow Press, 2006.

Recchia, Edward. "An Eye for an I: Adapting Henry James's 'The Turn of the Screw' to the Screen." *Literature Film Quarterly* 15 (1987), 28–35.

Rupprecht, Philip. *Britten's Musical Language*. Cambridge: Cambridge University Press, 2001.

Tintner, Adeline R. *Henry James's Legacy: The Afterlife of His Figure and Fiction* (Baton Rouge, LA: Louisiana State University Press, 1998). A large and unique work showing how James himself was represented in works by others (including caricaturists), and then how his works influenced other writers throughout the century who extended, rewrote, or differently set or solved James's fiction. She considers both fictional versions and film versions.

Wilson, Val. "Black and White and Shades of Grey: Ambiguity in *The Innocents*." In John R. Bradley, ed., *Henry James on Stage and Screen*. New York: Palgrave, 2000, 103–18.

INDEX

.